Maureen Allesee
Thanksgiving
1983

W9-CKH-003

Headbirths
or
The Germans
Are Dying Out

By the same author

The Tin Drum
Cat and Mouse
Dog Years
The Plebeians Rehearse the Uprising
Four Plays
Speak Out!
Local Anaesthetic
Max: A Play
From the Diary of a Snail
Inmarypraise
In the Egg and Other Poems
The Flounder
The Meeting at Telgte

Günter Grass

Headbirths
or
The Germans
Are Dying Out

Translated by Ralph Manheim

A Helen and Kurt Wolff Book

Harcourt Brace Jovanovich, Publishers

New York and London

For Nicolas Born

Copyright © 1980 by Hermann Luchterhand Verlag,
Darmstadt and Neuwied
English translation copyright © 1982
by Harcourt Brace Jovanovich, Inc.

All rights reserved. No part of this publication
may be reproduced or transmitted in any form or
by any means, electronic or mechanical, including
photocopy, recording, or any information storage
and retrieval system, without permission in
writing from the publisher.

Requests for permission to make copies of any
part of the work should be mailed to: Permissions,
Harcourt Brace Jovanovich, Publishers, 757 Third Avenue,
New York, N.Y. 10017

Library of Congress Cataloging in Publication Data

Grass, Günter, 1927–
    Headbirths, or, The Germans are dying out.

    Translation of: Kopfgeburten.
    I. Title. II. Title: Headbirths.
PT2613.R338K613   833'.914   81-48012
ISBN 0-15-139600-0   AACR2

Printed in the United States of America

First edition

B C D E

Publisher's Note

Headbirths was written in late 1979, shortly after Günter Grass returned from a trip to China and just before the German elections of 1980. Candidates of the two major parties contending for power were Helmut Schmidt, the Social Democrat Chancellor of the German Federal Republic, and Franz Josef Strauss, Bavarian Prime Minister and head of the opposition party, the Christian Democrats. Günter Grass's commitment was and is to the Social Democrats and their party head, Willy Brandt.

Headbirths
or
The Germans
Are Dying Out

I

Pedestrians among bicycle riders repeating one another ad infinitum in dress and bearing, immersed in a jungle of bicycle riders in Shanghai, the city where eleven out of nine hundred fifty million Chinese live, foreign bodies in the mass, we were suddenly hit by an idea, a speculative reversal: what if, from this day on, the world had to face up to the existence of nine hundred fifty million Germans, whereas the Chinese nation numbered barely eighty million, that is, the present population of the two Germanys. And a moment later I was confronted by the image of a hundred million Saxons and a hundred twenty million Swabians emigrating to offer the world their tight-packed industriousness.

In the midst of the cycling multitudes we were seized with terror. Is such a thought possible? Is such a thought permissible? Is such a world conceivable, a world inhabited by nine hundred fifty million Germans, who, even if the rate of increase is kept down to a bare 1.2 percent, will nevertheless multiply to something over one billion two hundred million Germans by the year 2000? Could the world bear it? Wouldn't the world have to defend itself (but how?) against such a multitude? Or could the world put up with as many Germans (Saxons and Swabians included) as there are Chinese today?

And what plausible cause could there be for such proliferation? Under what conditions, after what final victory might the Germans have multiplied so terrifyingly? By naturalization of all Nordics, Germanization, the mother cult, state nurseries?

To keep from losing myself in further inferences, I comfort myself with the thought that reviving Prussian traditions might make it possible to administer a billion Germans, just as the Chinese bureaucratic tradition makes it possible, despite revolutionary jolts, to administer the Chinese masses.

At that point Ute and I were forced back to reality, namely, the bicycle traffic. (I managed just in time to avoid my epiphany as an eternal pedestrian amid multitudes of German bicycle riders.) We escaped safe and sound from the traffic and other upsetting phenomena. — But when our month's journey brought us home from China via Singapore, Manila, and Cairo to Berlin, German reality was also shot through with speculations, these of a retrograde character.

Percentages were being argued about. The Christian opposition was attacking the government for preventing the Germans from multiplying properly. Citizen production, it was claimed, was stagnating, and Socialist-Liberal mismanagement was to blame. The German nation was threatened with extinction. The help of foreigners was needed to maintain the figure of sixty million. Disgraceful. Because if you reckoned without the foreigners—which was the only natural and obvious thing to do—you could predict first the slow, then the more and more rapid senescence of the German people, ultimately followed by their

4

total extinction, just as, conversely, the astronomic in-crease of the Chinese population was known in advance and has been reliably computed up to the year 2000.

The state visit of some top-level officials from the People's Republic of China, which took place while the Bundestag and the public were debating about the decline in the German population, may have contributed to the opposition's fears. At present this same opposition is man-ufacturing fear. And since fear in Germany has always had √ a high rate of increment and multiplies more quickly than do the Chinese, it has provided fear-mongering politicians with a program.

The Germans are dying out. Living space without people. Is such a thought possible? Is such a thought per-missible? What would the world be like without Germans? Would it have to look to the Chinese for salvation? Would the other nations of the earth find things lacked salt? Would a world without us have any meaning or savor? Would the world not be obliged to invent new Germans, including Saxons and Swabians? And mightn't the extinct Germans be more comprehensible in retrospect, since they would then be displayed in vitrines: free at last from unrest?

And another question: isn't there a certain grandeur in stepping out of history, in forgoing progeny, turning into a mere object of study for younger nations? Since this speculation promises to be long-lived, I have taken it as a subject. For a book or a film? I don't know yet. The title of the film or book or both might be *Headbirths*, harking √ back to the god Zeus, from whose head the goddess Athene was born: a paradox that has impregnated male minds to this day.

In my luggage I had yet another subject. Worked up in a fourteen-page manuscript and, what's more, put into

English: "The Two German Literatures"—or, as it might have been subtitled: "Germany, a Literary Concept." My thesis, you see, which I intended to expound in Peking, Shanghai, and elsewhere, was this: The one thing that can still reasonably be termed "all-German" in the two Germanys is literature. Though obstructed by the border, it doesn't stop at the border. This is a truth that the Germans don't want, or aren't allowed, to know. Since politically, ideologically, economically, and militarily the two Germanys live more against than alongside each other, they seem unable to see themselves simply as a nation: as two states forming one nation. And since, on a purely materialistic plane, one state "lives it up," and the other "defines itself," the alternative possibility of becoming a cultural nation is closed to them. Capitalism and communism are all they can think of. They like to compare prices, that's all.

Only lately, since the birth rate has got out of balance and the precious oil has stopped flowing freely, has there been a search for positive contents: extra sustenance to fill the material vacuum. The Germans rummage about for spiritual values which, to exclude intellectual refinements, they call fundamental values. Ethical concepts on clearance. Every day a new idea of Christ is thrown on the market. Culture is in. Readings, lectures, exhibitions are taken by storm. Perpetual theater festivals. Music ad nauseam. Like a drowning man, the citizen grasps at books. The writers of one and the other German state are more popular than the police of the one permit or than the pollsters of the other acknowledge; this frightens the poets.

I was planning to speak in simple, simplistic sentences about the phase-delayed development of German-language postwar literature, its clumsy directness and niggardly narrowness. Addressing two hundred (out of nine hundred

6

fifty million) Chinese in Peking, I said: "In 1945, Germany was not only militarily defeated. Not only the cities and industrial plants had been destroyed. Worse damage had been done: National Socialist ideology had robbed the German language of its meaning, had corrupted it and laid waste whole fields of words. In this mutilated language, writers, handicapped by its injuries, began to stammer more than write. Their helplessness was measured against Thomas Mann and Brecht, the giants of refugee literature; measured against their already classical greatness, only stammering could assert itself."

At this point, one of the small number of Chinese who had been allowed to assemble said: "That is our situation today. The Gang of Four"—he meant the Cultural Revolution—"cheated us out of ten years. We don't know anything. We're stupid. Everything, even the classics, was forbidden. And they crippled the language, too. Now a few writers are cautiously beginning stammering, as you put it—to write about reality. To deal with subjects that were forbidden: love and that sort of thing. Naturally in unphysical terms. In that respect we are still pretty strict. I don't have to tell you that we are not allowed to marry until late. Of course, there are reasons: the population problem. There are quite a lot of us, aren't there? And only married couples are given contraceptives. No one so far has written about the privation of the young. No place of their own. They can't make love."

The man who said this, in standard blues, seemed to be in his early thirties. He had learned his German during and in spite of the Cultural Revolution, out of textbooks that he was obliged to camouflage with the usual ideological dust jackets. After the fall of the Gang of Four, he was allowed to spend a year in Heidelberg, where he learned to speak like a West German. "We," he said, "our generation, I mean, have been really stultified." Today he's a teacher and trying to continue his education. "There's quite a lot of class time now. Thirty-eight hours a week."

My teacher couple—this headbirth—come from Itzehoe, a district capital in Holstein, between marshland and heathland, with declining population and increasing modernization damage. He is in his middle, she in her early thirties. He was born in Hademarschen, where his mother is still living, she in Krempe, where her parents, after selling the farm, have gone into retirement. Both are indefatigably self-reflecting veterans of the student protest movement. They met in Kiel, at a sit-in against the Vietnam War or the Springer press or both. I say Kiel tentatively. It could have been Hamburg or Berlin. Ten years ago they tried, with a great many words, to "destroy what is destroying us." What violence they went in for was confined to objects. *Their* cultural revolution petered out more quickly. Consequently, they were able to complete their teacher-training course without appreciable delay and, after a short period of swapping partners in communes, to get married: no minister, just the family.

That was seven years ago. For five and four years they have been employed in the state school system, having passed both first and second state examinations. Their mutual love on a fairly even keel. A model couple. A couple with many duplicates. A couple straight out of a contemporary picture book. They keep a cat and still have no child.

Not because they can't or because it doesn't take, but because when she finally decides she wants one "after all," he says "not yet," whereas when he opts for a child—"It seems feasible, theoretically"—she counters, as though responding to a cue, with: "Not to me. Or not any more. If we're to act responsibly, we must take an objective view. What sort of future are you going to let a child loose in?

8

What prospects will it have? Anyway, there are enough children already, too many. In India, Mexico, Egypt, China. Look at the statistics."

They both teach foreign languages—he English, she French—at the Kaiser Karl School, KKS for short, and geography as a second subject. The Kaiser Karl School is so called because in the ninth century Charlemagne [in German Karl der Grosse, Charles the Great] sent a punitive expedition to Holstein, which walled itself in approximately where Itzehoe is falling apart today. And since they are both particularly fond of teaching geography, they are up not only on rivers, mountains, ore deposits, and the chemistry of soils, but also on population figures. He quotes Marx on the capitalist law of accumulation through redundancy, she harps on data, curves, computer projections: "Here, look at South America. Everywhere a three-percent increase. Five in Mexico. What little progress there is, they eat it up. And the Pope, the idiot, still interdicts the pill."

She takes it regularly. Always at the start of her first class. A kink, or call it a kinky demonstration of her rationalized self-denial. So this is how the *Headbirths* movie could begin: Long shot of the Indian subcontinent. She, cut off at the waist, covering half the Bay of Bengal, all Calcutta, and Bangladesh, casually takes the pill, slaps a book shut (she is not wearing glasses), and says, "It is safe to say that birth control as a means of family planning has been a failure in India."

Then she might question the class, which is offscreen, about population figures and overspill in the states of Bihar, Kerala, and Uttar Pradesh: India's misery reeled off in figures. Destitution as a course of study. The future.

Which explains why I said to Volker Schlöndorff, whom we met with Margarethe von Trotta in Djakarta and later in Cairo, "If we do this picture, we should shoot it in India or in Java or—now that I've been there—in China, if they let us."

The idea is for our teacher couple to take a trip, the way Ute and I, Volker and Margarethe take trips. And, like us, standing there alien and sweating, they compare the reality with the statistics. The leap through the air from Itzehoe to Bombay. The jet lag. The skimmed guidebooks in their hand luggage. The preconceived knowledge. The inoculations. The new arrogance: We've come to learn. . . .

Yet they smell pungently of fear. In the swarming center of Bombay they could (like me in Shanghai) be hit by speculations: suppose the world had to face up to the existence of seven hundred million Germans instead of Indians. But this in-between figure doesn't suit us. To a German mind it's not speculative enough. Either we die out or we swell to a billion. Either/Or.

The Schlöndorffs and we are traveling professionally, for "Goethe."* Despite the heavy program, it's simpler. They show their films, I read from my books. Bent on an information-gathering vacation, our teacher couple sign up with a travel agency, whose prospectus promises "reality-oriented tours." I already know how "Goethe" operates; I'll have to dream up the travel agency (and its "crash program"). We are dependent on the heads of the Goethe Institutes; our couple will follow a paid guide, who knows everything: where to buy Ganesh figurines or Javanese marionettes, that lateral head movements mean "yes" in India, what to eat, what not to eat, how much to tip ricksha men, and whether, when the two of them—accompanied, it goes without saying, by a remunerated

---

* The Goethe Institutes, German cultural institutes abroad, had sponsored Grass and Schlöndorff (who directed the film of *The Tin Drum*) on a reading and lecturing tour of China and India. —Ed.

native—are visiting some slum, it's all right to photograph the slum dwellers.

Not a word about the heads of the Goethe Institutes and their private manias. About our paid guide, who has studied Hindu civilization for the film we are planning to make, this much can be said: possibly a senescent baby face. His watery gaze suggests the long view. A sort of God figure in nickel-rimmed glasses. With two opinions about everything.

Like us. On the one hand, nuclear power plants represent an incalculable risk; on the other hand, only the new technology can guarantee the standard of living to which we are accustomed. On the one hand, manual farming provides food and employment for eight hundred million Chinese peasants; on the other hand, only mechanized farming methods can increase the yield per acre, thus on the one and on the other hand condemning half the peasantry to unemployment or releasing them for other, as yet unspecified, tasks. On the one hand, the slums of Bangkok, Bombay, Manila, and Cairo should be sanitized; on the other hand, sanitized slums encourage more and more peasants to leave the land for the cities. On the one and on the other hand.

Our teacher couple from Itzehoe—which is near Brokdorf—are politically, personally, and generally cut out for the Central European "Ontheonehand-ontheotherhand" parlor game. She belongs to the FDP (Free Democrats); he lectures about the Third World at SPD (Social Democratic) meetings. Both say, "On the one hand, the environmentalists are right; on the other, they'll get Strauss elected."

This, and still more, is almost too much for the mind to bear. He deplores the lack of long-range views, she the lack of meaning in general. Her moods, his afternoon slump. She blames her father for "selling off the farm to the egg industry"; he would really like his mother, who is living on her own in Hademarschen, to move into their apartment, but he is being "sensible," as he puts it, and looking around for a well-run old-people's home. She, who is basically committed to motherhood, believes herself, now that her geography program is burdened with the Indian subcontinent, in duty bound to forgo children. He, who regards his schoolchildren as enough and by the end of the week more than enough, has said recently, "Anyway, even if Mother moves in, our prewar apartment with garden privileges is big enough for three."

They don't make things easy for themselves. The child is always present. Whether they are shopping at Itzehoe's Holstein Shopping Center or standing on the Elbe dike at Brokdorf, bedded on their double mattress or looking for a new second-hand car: the child always joins in the conversation, makes eyes at baby clothes, wants to crawl on the Elbe beach, longs at ovulation time for the sprinkling that fructifies, and demands auto doors with childproof locks. But they never get beyond the whatif or supposingthat stage, and Harm's mother (as surrogate child) is alternately moved to their apartment and shipped to an old-people's home, until some forenoon shock derails their single-tracked dialogue.

When in geography class Dörte Peters advocates family planning, ranging from birth control to voluntary sterilization, as a cure for overpopulation, a girl student (as blond as Dörte Peters) jumps up. Protest makes her beautiful: "But what about us? No more babies. Fewer and fewer Germans. Why have we stopped having children? Why? In India, Mexico, China, they're multiplying like mad. And we here, we Germans are dying out!"

Schlöndorff and I don't know yet how the class reacts

to this indictment. Is this outbreak attributable to the student's home environment? Mightn't it be better for one of the boy pupils to take a pot shot at the foreign workers: "Practically no umbilical cords are being severed in Itzehoe except among the Turks!" Or should boy and girl alternate their crescendo of diatribes?

In any case, the assertion that the "Germans are dying out!" propagates (after a brief outburst of student laughter, quickly broken off in dismay) that fear which invades even the secondary-school teacher Dörte Peters, and which, mixed with other fears, will fuel slogans that Franz Josef Strauss will mouth or cause to be mouthed well into the coming election year.

"Another difficulty," I said to Schlöndorff. "If we want to shoot this picture in 1980, the only possible time is July–August. Any earlier or later, the election campaign will be going on. I don't know what you're going to do. But the sidelines aren't good enough for me. Too many people might be wanting to indulge their little craving for doom."

At Peking University and the Shanghai Foreign Language Institute, no one inquired about German reunification plans in which the People's Republic of China might play a part. And I don't know whether my contention that one cultural nation embracing two German states is the only sort of unification that remains possible, met with any more interest than it does at home. I said: "Our neighbors ✓ in the East and West will never again tolerate a concentration of economic and military power in the center of Europe, where two world wars were started. But the existence of two German states under the roof of a common culture might be acceptable to our neighbors and compatible with the national sentiment of the German people."

One more illusion? A writer's fantasy? Is my thesis—

which like some crackpot itinerant preacher I propounded in Peking and Shanghai and later elsewhere—that German writers have shown themselves to be better patriots than their separatist rulers a mere gesture of defiance? Citing examples from Logau and Lessing and from Biermann and Böll, I naïvely (touching, perhaps, in my naïveté) presupposed some knowledge of German culture and its development. (Even my two teachers, whom I've named Harm and Dörte Peters, shake their heads: I'm asking too much of them. "Man," says Harm, "that stuff is unknown except on the Third Program.")

He who returns home finds—himself. Along with the official visit from China and the fear that the Germans would die out, along with Bahro's* move from East to West and the nightly viewing of Cambodian genocide on TV, the after-pains of the Frankfurt Book Fair were the order of the day when we got back. Time and time again for the last thirty years, as long as one German state has existed side by side with another, a compelling need has been felt to extract the National Socialist past of such men as Adenauer's Minister Globke, as Chancellor Kiesinger, Prime Minister Filbinger, and the present President Carstens, from files that had somehow (as though of their own volition) got mislaid. Under the headline "We Will Go On Writing When Everything Has Fallen into Ruins," the weekly *Die Zeit* has published an article claiming that German postwar literature began not in 1945, as generally supposed, but during the Nazi period.

This article provoked a controversy that is still dragging on. Far be it from me to impugn the chastity of post-

---

* Rudolf Bahro published a "reformist" book in the West, while living in East Germany. He was brought to trial, imprisoned, and finally allowed to leave for West Germany. —ED.

war literature, and in particular of those writers who stayed in Germany during the Third Reich and continued to publish their works in the area of captive freedom the Nazis had set aside for them; but because these theses that had sparked off the controversy were loaded with partly true and therefore inaccurate hints purporting to prove that certain writers had been more or less close to National Socialist institutions, the central question is now being treated as an incidental, while impressive energies are thrown into the attacks to which the author of the controversial article has laid himself open.

Branded as an informer. An enemy to be wiped out. In the cold scrap heap he has found a piece of hot iron and picked it up, picked it up in public. Fair game, he doubles back like a hare. How much longer? Infringement of a taboo is ritually punished.

Whenever Germans—culprits or victims, accusers or accused, the guilty or the innocents born later—bite into their past, they take deeply ingrained positions, they know they are right and that everyone else is wrong. Unthinkingly—and mistakenly—they revive the German past; a wound is reopened, and the healing time that has intervened is annulled. I don't except myself. As if I had taken my burden of German problems to Asia with me, toted them as far as Peking, I asked my Chinese colleagues (over tea and goodies) how they deal with the writers who committed themselves for twelve years to counterrevolution, to the Gang of Four. With the circumlocutions customary in their country, they replied: During the bad years literature was forbidden. Nothing could thrive in the icy wind. Just one author, a favorite of the Gang of Four, was allowed to fill the playbill of the Peking Opera, which had previously been swept bare, with eight of his plays. Actually, the man is still a member of the Society of Authors. He will go on being a member, and in the meantime he has written a ninth play. Like the others, it is dramatically effective. A great talent. One can talk with him.

In both German states his expulsion from the Society of Authors would have been demanded. (We do not wish, they told me politely in Peking, to repeat the errors of the Gang of Four.) What errors, and whose, do we repeat?

My teacher couple from Itzehoe on the Stör were born after the war; he in '45, she in '48. His father was killed shortly before the end in the Battle of the Bulge. Her father returned from a Soviet prison camp in '47: a prematurely aged young farmer. Since Harm and Dörte have not known fascism, the word springs more quickly to their lips than either is prepared to tolerate in the other. Such a handy word. Always fits a little. Fills the mouth and hisses like the candidate's name [Strauss].

"No," says Harm. "He's no fascist."

"Well, then, an unconscious one," says Dörte. "Otherwise he wouldn't be in such a hurry when contradicted to strike back with 'Fascists! Red fascists!'" They settle for "latent."

They'll be packing their bags soon. Light summer clothes, cotton, tropical wear. They still need a few injections, still have to pay farewell visits to Harm's mother and Dörte's parents and make arrangements for the cat. They couldn't come to terms with themselves or with their reciprocally affirmed and negated desire for a child, and since even teachers find the summer holidays long, Harm and Dörte have decided on a trip to India, Thailand, and Indonesia—or to China, in case Schlöndorff and I get permission to shoot our picture there.

16

2

The fight goes on. I've joined in. It concerns me. Names that are important to me have been named: Eich and Huchel, Koeppen and Kästner.* I don't know what made them decide to survive in their fashion. I can't judge their conduct during the Nazi period (their continuing to write and to publish), but I assume that each one for himself (and Eich and Huchel in conflict with each other) measured his conduct in comparison with the fate of those who were forced to leave Germany and of those who were driven to suicide or murdered. Or they were obliged later on to measure themselves by those authors who had also stayed and survived, but without making use of the captive freedom shrewdly granted by the Nazis.

I will not judge. A dubious stroke of luck, my birth year of 1927, forbids me to condemn anyone. I was too young to be seriously put to the test. But it touched me all the same. At the age of thirteen I took part in a contest organized by the Hitler Youth magazine *Lend a Hand*

---

* German poets and novelists. —Ed.

[*Hilf mit*]. I started writing at an early age, and appreciation meant a lot to me. But, evidently misjudging the judges, I sent in some sort of melodramatic fragment about the Kashubians. A surefire guarantee that I'd be lucky enough not to win a Hitler Youth *Lend a Hand* prize.

I got off easy. Spotless record. No tangible facts to my discredit. Yet my imagination, which refuses to keep quiet, can supply quite a few: I backdate myself. Suppose I make my biography start ten years earlier. What's ten years? A mere nothing. My imagination can do it.

So I was born in 1917. In 1933 I'd have been sixteen and not six; at the outbreak of the war twenty-two and not twelve. Subject to immediate call-up, I would probably, like most of my age group, have been killed in the war. But despite this likelihood, there is no reason (other than preference) to suppose that I would not have developed unswervingly into a convinced National Socialist. Coming from a petit-bourgeois family that repressed its half-Kashubian origins, brought up on German idealism and drilled in the principle of German purity, I would have been susceptible to geopolitical enthusiasm and would have given ear to those who (in the name of the nation) justified subjective wrong as objective right. (Although, or because, my uncle Franz worked at the Polish post office, the Danzig SS–Home Guard could have counted on my services in the late summer of 1939, or at least on the support of my pen.)

Thanks to my dowry, my relentless literary talent, movement-related events (the seizure of power, Harvest Thanksgiving Day, the Führer's birthday) would have prompted me to rhapsodic verse, all the more so since the politics of the Hitler Youth (see Anacker, Schirach, Baumann, Menzel*) allowed for Late Expressionist word con-

---

* Writers, poets, ideologists supporting the Nazi doctrines. —ED.

flations and sweeping metaphors. My contributions to Morning Celebrations are perfectly imaginable. Or—aroused by sensitive German teachers, a nature-worshipping inwardness would have made me meek and mawkish and guided me in Carossa's or, even more meekly, Wilhelm Lehmann's traces: summer's radiance, autumn's bounty, always in busy pursuit of the seasons. In either case, whether stationed at the Atlantic Wall, on Oslo Fjord, or the myth-haunted coast of Crete, or assigned (as befits a volunteer raised in a seaport) to a submarine, I would (as I know myself) have looked for a publisher and found one.

Beginning with Stalingrad—I would then have been twenty-six, a lieutenant if not a corporal—a murky light would have dawned on me. Quite possibly involved in the shooting of partisans, in punitive expeditions and clean-up operations, as eyewitness to deportations of Jews too patent to overlook, I'd have mingled new tones—vague melancholy, words chosen in despair, somber ambiguities—with my Late Expressionist rhymes or invocations of bulrushes. During the retreat (in contrast to my literary phase during the period of territory-devouring victories), I would probably have turned out so-called "poetry of lasting significance."

And on this stylistic level, which in 1944 would still have been acceptable to my publisher and the censors, I (if still alive) would have had no trouble living through the unconditional surrender, Germany's "fresh start," and a possible two years of imprisonment, and would have gone over to the new, jejune, undernourished, pacifist, or even antifascist ideas—as we read in a hundred and more biographies.

As far as I know, only one man, Wolfgang Weyrauch, admitted to such a biography. I follow him with my headbirth: yes, it's true. For us there was no fresh start or zero

19

point. The transitions were muddily fluid. Overwhelming horror at the extent of the crimes one had tolerated and directly or indirectly abetted, for which in any case one must share responsibility, came only later, several years after the alleged fresh start, when things were beginning to look up. This horror will endure.

That is why I have joined in the fight. Once again we are so fair-minded. With democratic guile we undercut our misgivings. We find far too many things understandable. We call the brutal will to power "vital." We forgive the outbursts of a man whose vocabulary embraces every known calumny. We say: That's his Bavarian temperament. We call our cowardly cringing "liberal." The radio and television studios are already being furnished for the inner emigration. All you have to do is take a trip and return home: the old, forever new, horror will be there.

In addition to my lecture on "The German Literatures" and my novel *The Flounder*, I took three pages of jottings on the *Headbirths* theme along with me on our Asian trip. In every city we stopped in I read simple chapters from *The Flounder*: how Amanda Woyke introduced the potato into Prussia. This eighteenth-century fairy tale is timely in present-day Asia, in regions, for instance, where attempts to complement the exclusive cultivation of rice with other crops (maize, soybeans) are frustrated by the obstinate resistance of the peasants, until a Chinese or Javanese Amanda Woyke . . .

I read my notes on *Headbirths* during the outbound flight and larded them with additions. But not until my return to the narrows of German life do my slips fall out of my portfolio: my teacher couple from Itzehoe, Dörte and Harm Peters, have survived my evasions and counterprojects. They're still getting ready for their trip.

She wants to concentrate on just India. "Otherwise

we'll spread ourselves too thin and we won't get anything out of it."

He insists on visiting an old school friend on Bali. "I'm interested to know how he feels, living there. And we have to relax some of the time. Besides, they say it's beautiful. So unspoiled."

She waits until the last day of school before mentioning her plans to her class (after distributing the report cards—two pupils left behind): "You know, I've been thinking of a study trip, to India and so on. Maybe in the fall I'll be able to treat the problems of overpopulation more graphically, on the basis of my own observation, I mean."

He questions his class: "We studied Indonesia recently. My wife and I are going to visit Java and Bali during the summer holidays. What in particular should I watch for? Any questions?"

One of the students replies, "How much do Japanese motorcycles cost there?"

And later, in Djakarta, Harm Peters asks a Chinese dealer the price of a Kawasaki in rupees, so as to be able, toward the end of the film, to give this student (who is interested in nothing else) a pedagogically motivated answer: It costs so-and-so much, or so-and-so-many marks, which, for an Indonesian worker who makes only so-and-so much, comes to more than five months' wages, whereas a West German wage earner . . .

In another scene, Harm Peters, a member of the Social Democratic Party, is giving a lecture. After dealing with the local items on the agenda, he speaks (possibly backed up by slides) on the problems of the Asian slums and, referring to his impending trip to Asia, promises to treat the same problems "in depth" on his return. But when Harm Peters throws the meeting open for discussion, a metalworker brushes the lecturer's problems aside:

"Let's get back for a moment to point three on the agenda. Are we getting that street lamp outside the vocational school, or aren't we?"

When Peters insists on a discussion relevant to his lecture—"Comrades, we were talking about the problems of the Third World!"—he is beaten back from all sides. "Sure. But we're worried about the safety of our school-children. That's important, too. Naturally you don't understand. You have no children."

At this point the film should pick up the cue. The year before, when Dörte (as now) on the one hand wanted a child but on the other hand was unwilling to bring a child, "my child, into a world increasingly contaminated by nuclear radiation," she had herself aborted in the second month. Harm thought she was doing the right thing: "When you are really committed to motherhood, when the Landtag elections are behind us, then and only then . . ."

On the Elbe dike between Hollerwettern and Brokdorf, they discuss this and the world's other miseries. Their raised vantage point overlooks a construction site protected by walls, fences, chevaux-de-frise, miradors, and more such borrowings from the German Democratic Republic, but grown to weeds and beginning to look almost idyllic since work on the Brokdorf nuclear power station was stopped by a court order, which will most likely be countermanded at the next session of the Schleswig district court.

Harm says: "Evasions, cheap evasions. One day it's the population explosion in the Third World, one day it's the impending Landtag elections, another time it's my mother, who has no intention of moving in with us, and if nothing better turns up, it's some nuclear power plant being planned here or somewhere else that stops us from bringing a child, our child, into the world."

But Dörte just can't help having these varying fears

for the future: "If we ourselves have no future to look forward to, how, I ask you, can you expect a child, our child..."

Harm waxes cynical: "Fast Breeders Bar Offspring! That could be a headline in the *Bild-Zeitung*. And who's going to pay for our pensions when we get old? After the pork mountain and the butter mountain, weren't we supposed to get an old-folks' mountain...?"

"But I don't want a child!" she shouts.

"Because it might put a crimp in your plans!" he shouts.

Maybe at this point Dörte laughs rather reluctantly, but she admits: "All right. Of course convenience has something to do with it. But not only for me. Your way of life doesn't allow for a child, either. Your independence. Your love of travel and all that. I mean, once we've got the child..."

Harm stands on the dike like a pastor on a fast day, preaching more to the cows and sheep in the meadow and the giant tankers on the Elbe than to his Dörte. "Verily I say unto you, your sacred right to self-realization is in danger. Could we, dearest Dörte, take our carefully planned trip to Asia with a baby on our necks? Mustn't we stop to ask ourselves whether our program, which promises not only the usual sights, but also, and I quote, 'the often cruel realities of Asia as well,' is compatible with the presence of a sweet little cherub in our hand luggage? Does Dörte Peters wish, for instance, to drag her baby to India, where there are already so many, so far too many babies? And what shall we have our son, if it turns out to be a son, inoculated against? Smallpox, cholera, yellow fever? Should it, like us, for three weeks before leaving, ingurgitate malaria tablets or have them stirred into its sterile canned food? And wouldn't we be obliged to take along all that disposable rubbish—fifty vacuum-sealed cans, innumerable packages, bags, diapers, a sterilizer, a baby scale, and God knows what else—so our little boy . . ."

This time Dörte's laugh is really a bit too loud. And just as spontaneously, she can take the contrary view. "But I want a child, I want a child! I want to be pregnant, fat, round, cow-eyed. And go 'moo.' Do you hear? Moo! And this time, my dear Harm, father of my planned child, we're not calling it off after two months. So help me. As soon as we're airborne, hear, as soon as we have all this here, that's right, as soon as we have you jugheads over there in your atomic concentration camp below us and behind us, I'm going off the pill!"

The director's instructions are roughly: Both laugh. But because the camera is still on them, they do more than laugh. They grab hold of each other, roughhouse, peel each other's jeans off, "fuck," as Harm says, "screw," as Dörte says, each other on the dike among cows and sheep, under the open sky. A few guards at the still-future construction site of the Brokdorf nuclear power plant may be watching them, no one else. Then two low-flying pursuit planes. ("Shit on NATO!" Dörte moans.) In the distance, ships on the Elbe at high tide.

A note on one of the slips that I took with me to Asia and then home again says, "Shortly before landing in Bombay or Bangkok—breakfast has been cleared away— Dörte takes the pill." Harm, who only seems to be asleep, sees her and accepts it with fatalism.

This is going too fast. Before I make the two of them take off, I want to maintain uncertainty for a little while. They haven't settled on a program. There are so many, too many, travel prospectuses. None is right for headbirths. True to my title, I have to dream up a prospectus. One for the future. Because tomorrow, slum tourism will be a possibility. Fed up with the usual sights, we want to see at last

24

what no postcard knows, what ails the world, what our tax money goes for, to see how people live in the slums: merrily, it would seem, as the illustrated brochures show, for all their destitution.

The offerings of a travel agency calling itself Sisyphus strike Harm and Dörte as "pretty brutal." (Why Sisyphus? I'll think about that later.)

She says, "Man, are they cynical!"

He says, "But honest."

The spiel in the brochure is aimed at an untapped market. "People wishing to push the stone, strong enough to see and understand profoundly troubling truths, people intent on facts, including hard ones . . ." So it goes, in sober typescript, followed by succinct information about infant mortality in Southeast Asia, population density and per-capita income in Java. Sisyphus has computed for its clients the protein deficiency prevailing in each locality and noted next to it (a statistical indictment) the rising price of soybeans at the Chicago Board of Trade.

"That's the stuff," says Harm. "They realize that our kind of people are looking for an alternative program. We want to confront reality, not let ourselves be driven like cattle through temple grounds. Here you have it in black and white: 'See the real, unvarnished Asia.' "

After a brief flurry of indignation "because they're out to make a pile of money like everyone else," Dörte finds the proffered travel program well balanced: "They haven't neglected the cultural aspect, either. And here and there they give you a bit of vacation fun."

I don't except myself from having such mixed needs. Ute and I traveled in pretty much the same way, though without a prospectus. In the morning we'd visit some slum, at noon we'd rest in an air-conditioned hotel, in the late afternoon visit Buddhist temple grounds, in the evening (after my compulsory lecture) listen over drinks and snacks to a report drawn up by some experts about a famine-stricken region some two hundred miles distant, which we—sympathetic, humbly superior, taking the aloof interest of foreigners, straining to ward off nausea—were to visit the following day. During the outbound flight, I had cast off my statistical knowledge and resolved to be receptive, a sponge. Seldom asking questions, I heard, saw, smelled, and I took no notes. And photographs, which came into being incidentally—one might almost say accidentally—were not taken into consideration afterward. I was ashamed of my shamelessness. Now I want to send Harm and Dörte on our trip, but they argue with me. They don't want to cast off their previous knowledge. They think I have my nerve with me. They still have inhibitions about traveling in accordance with my mixed program. They're embarrassed. But since they don't want to be common tourists and, as they both say, feel sure of their "objective judgment," they—Dörte before Harm—sign the Sisyphus form; before they've even packed their bags, their trip has started.

I don't know yet how my misgivings and excuses can be shown in a medium—film—that makes everything clear and simple. Even if they have signed, booked passage, and decided in favor of my itinerary, I have my doubts. I'll have to talk it over with Schlöndorff. Nothing but mental states and changes of place—what other action have Harm and Dörte to offer? Except for their Yes-to-baby No-to-baby, nothing exciting happens between them. At the most, Harm's desire to visit a school friend by the name of Uwe Jensen on Bali might bring in some action.

Because, you see, Uwe has a sister, whose name is Monika, living in Itzehoe. She (and not Harm's mother in Hademarschen) is taking care of the cat. She fishes her brother's address out of a pile of letters. "This last thing," she says, "dates from two years ago. Here's what it says: 'Getting along fine. Just wish I had something juicy to eat.' " And Monika Steppuhn—her husband is a printer, employed by Gruner and Jahr—reminds Harm of his school friend's gourmandise: "Man, remember the time in Brunsbüttel after the bicycle tour when Uwe shoveled in five portions of calf's feet with fried potatoes. . . ."

So Harm goes to a butcher shop in Itzehoe and buys a kilo of coarse, homemade, lightly smoked liver sausage in natural casing, which, because of the climate awaiting it, he has sealed in plastic. "I'm sure it will make Uwe happy," he says to Dörte. "You can't get it down there. And I remember like it was yesterday how he loved liver sausage."

The vacuum-packed liver sausage is later stowed in their hand luggage. Concerning this school friend, it might be divulged, in addition to his sporting prowess (hand-ball), that he made quick money as an agent for Hoechst or Siemens, first in Singapore, then in Djakarta—"He always had a head on his shoulders," says his sister—and then retired to Bali.

Harm and Dörte take their cat, gray on white paws, to the Steppuhns' in a basket. Erich, Monika's husband, doesn't think much of his widely traveled brother-in-law: "Irresponsible. And where he stands politically, God only knows."

Harm is delighted with his purchase. "Man, will he be surprised when we walk in with that sausage. I only hope the address is still the same." (The Steppuhns, too, are childless; they are pleased to have the borrowed cat.)

I admit that the idea of the liver sausage (as the basis of a subplot) is autobiographical. Shortly before we set out, the West German ambassador in Peking let us know that he was longing for some homemade coarse liver sausage. So we had Herr Köller, our village butcher in Wewelsfleth, seal two lightly smoked, tight-packed liver sausages in plastic, stowed these products of Holstein in our hand luggage, and flew them into the People's Republic of China. I am able to speak so freely because Ambassador Wickert is being retired in 1980, at which time he will be released from all diplomatic exigencies.

So the liver sausage is a fact and not a headbirth. And the joy that sausage aroused in Ambassador Wickert, the China hand and author, was a reality not allowed for in protocol. A man of military bearing, capable of mustering his very passions in parade formation. A Prussian conservative whom, after an evening's conversation about Chinese mentality and German absolutes, I succeeded in winning to my side for the forthcoming elections.

Maybe certain Prussian virtues, which might also be called Chinese virtues—punctilious punctuality, for instance—are worth reviving; for by the time we got back from Asia, Ambassador Wickert (under an impressive letterhead) had already thanked Butcher Köller for the coarse, lightly smoked liver sausage; as I, in turn, thank him for his plot-fostering idea, because it, the sausage, is now flying in a southwesterly direction with Harm and Dörte Peters. The tourist group to which they belong is awaited by a Dr. Konrad Wenthien, a tour guide in the employ of the Sisyphus Tourist Bureau.

Is this figure needed, and must he bear this name? Aren't we letting loose another cinematic notion that can hardly contribute to our central Yes-to-baby No-to-baby theme? And isn't it foreseeable that—if only on the basis of the flown-in liver sausage—an incidental, accidental, and ultimately conspiratorial relationship will develop between this Wenthien and our man on Bali, that is, the school friend Uwe?

This I shall try to prevent, even though Harm Peters, who reads little but when he does devours detective stories with passion, has a bent for adventurous flights of thought. (He is already beginning to suspect that the sausage is too long for its weight.) Nor shall I conceal the fact that Volker Schlöndorff, whose attention I called to Vicki Baum's novel *Love and Death on Bali,* recently made me a present of Eric Ambler's *Passage of Arms* in German translation, and that the English original of this thriller, which takes place in Hong Kong, Manila, Singapore, and Sumatra, is now included in Harm Peters's luggage.

I'm beginning to see the lure of writing for the movies. There's so much material lying around. Shots give birth to shots. Cut everything but the "action." Let the picture do the talking. Always keep the cutting room in mind. Picture language. Cut cut cut. Actually, I wanted to follow an entirely different lead, the initial idea that struck Ute and me like an epiphany in the middle of Shanghai, transmogrifying nine hundred and fifty million Chinese into something approaching a billion Germans who, because still divided, are searching for their national self-assessment—not on bicycles, to be sure, but motorized, every last one of them.

Eighty million restless Germans transformed into a billion Germans in a state of unrest. Among them the proportionate number of Saxons and Swabians. What a population explosion! An epic flare-up. A ferment. What makes them so restless? What are they looking for? God? The absolute number? The meaning behind meaning? Insurance against nothingness?

They want at last to know themselves. They ask themselves and, dangerously in need of help, ask their neighbors, who, measured against the German plethora, have shrunk to pygmy nations: Who are we? Where are we from? What makes us Germans? And what in God's name is Germany?

Since the Germans, even a billion strong, are as thorough as ever, they set up several deeply echeloned national commissions of inquiry, which work at cross purposes. Imagine the paper consumption, the jurisdictional disputes among the various provinces and Germanys. They're so intent on the organizational setup that they've already lost sight of its purpose.

Time for me. I speak up. But my early, pre-epiphanic suggestion that we should transcend all diversity and look upon ourselves as one cultural nation finds a hearing only in marginal zones. At the start my theses are discussed, singly and as a whole, only by the delegates of the culture-creating minority—twelve and a half million artists, including four hundred eighty-seven thousand writers. What is culture? What does it encompass? Is hygiene the culture of the body? And what, exactly what share of the GNP does culture represent?

But it is already foreseeable that powerful interest groups—not only the churches and labor unions, not only private and socialized industry, but also the numerically almost equivalent armed forces of the two German states— will soon regard themselves as bearers, and in the case of the élite formations even as creators, of culture. They aspire to embody the nation, and lay claim to the mission of defining it, of imbuing it with meaning. For where would we be if only artists, notoriously recalcitrant when it comes to organization, were entitled to speak in the name of the nation? I hear shouts of "Those individualists! Those welfare cases! Those visionaries! Always wanting special treatment. Acting as if they had taken out a lease on culture. What counts today in our, in one sense or another, democratic society is the subcultures of our steel mills or pool rooms, our subsidized mass cultures—get me! —and none of your élitist superstructural shit!"

This puts a crimp on my idea, which, I admit, was tailored for a mere eighty million Germans. I'll just have to leave a billion Germans to their unrest and alarming process of self-discovery. Singing—some briskly, some sadly —the German masses skedaddle into the blue distance.

But I still have Harm and Dörte left. In both cases I can see what I've got. I can count on their problem, because it's a headbirth. Now, shortly before the landing, she, contrary to her sworn intention—Yes-to-baby!—takes the pill—No-to-baby!—and now at last they land in Bombay with a kilo of German liver sausage in their hand luggage.

But since my intention to make them finally land is still blocked by misgivings based on details that had no place in the first draft, the question arises here in the third draft: mightn't it be better to buy the coarse liver sausage not from some butcher in the city of Itzehoe, with its population of barely thirty-four thousand, but at Kruse's Delicatessen on Kirchstrasse, across the street from the Church of St. Lawrence; from there it's only a few steps to Gerbers' Bookshop, where Harm buys his detective stories and Dörte her reading matter on "clean energy."

In and behind two overluxurious showcases, two white-smocked brothers see to it that Kruse's Delicatessen is always fully stocked. Such abundance could tempt Harm to buy a smoked goose breast in addition to the coarse liver sausage, but he confines himself to the plot-fostering sausage. In addition to paperbacks about India and Indonesia, Dörte could ask for some light exotic literature and Herr Gerbers in person could call her attention to Vicki Baum's *Love and Death on Bali*. But she confines herself to statistical material, because we don't want the novel to come up until later. And at this point it could be said that Itzehoe is not authentically on the Stör, because in 1974 the town fathers, succumbing to an attack of city planning, voted to fill in the loop in the Stör, which then passed through the New City. Another point in favor of Kruse's Delicatessen is that Feldschmiede, which branches off from Kirchstrasse, is now a pedestrian zone. Here one occasionally sees Comrade Harm Peters along with other comrades (Erich Steppuhn) handing out *The Red Fox*, organ of the Itzehoe Social Democrats. And it is expected that during the autumn phase of the election campaign, political meetings will be held in the Feldschmiede pedestrian zone, which leads to the Holstein Shopping Center.

Harm is on the editorial board of *The Red Fox*. At Gerbers' Dörte buys more than she can read. Itzehoe was founded in 1238. And the kilo of German liver sausage, which was bought at Kruse's Delicatessen and is now landing in Bombay with Harm and Dörte, is indeed a delicacy.

3

Another obstacle. They are still circling over Bombay without permission to land, because I forgot to inject something that's in my notes and should have been considered before the takeoff: the future.

Since Harm and Dörte Peters don't set out until the beginning of the summer holidays, the early-May elections for the North Rhine–Westphalia provincial diet have had results which are known to my teacher couple but not to me, and which I can't even guess at; just as the results of the provincial-diet elections in Baden-Württemberg (mid-March) are still a mystery to me as I write this. The democratic rosary. The ifs and buts. The future is making a fool of me. If the electoral percentages lead to a workable coalition of the Free Democrats with the Social Democrats, can't Strauss be expected to throw in the sponge, mutter "Nobody loves me" or something of the sort, and emigrate to Alaska?

O future! What would we do without him? Who could supplant his pithy bluntness? Who would provide images for our nightmares? How would I get on with my

Headbirths without him? The truth in tea leaves. What do I know? What *can* I know? I simply assume that North Rhine–Westphalia will run true to form and that Strauss will not drop out. Everything is still in the dark, Harm and Dörte fly through the air (and finally land) with the certainty of finding him, the home-grown apocalyptic, going strong when they return in the late summer.

Why Bombay? Of course Harm and Dörte could stop off in Thailand first; charter flights often make detours. Immediately after passport inspection, Dr. Wenthien the tour guide could take delivery of their little group and for the first time test the effect of his leitmotif: "Asia is different." Since our teacher couple have done their homework conscientiously and are eager to experience what contrasts Sisyphus has to offer, they wish not only to take in the art-historical sights (temples, temples!), Bangkok's picaresque thieves' market and a boat ride on the khlongs, but also to visit Klong Toei, the harborside slum mentioned in the travel brochure, a project that Dr. Wenthien regards as feasible, though entailing a small extra charge for native guidance, and interesting for its "social-reality content": "But I strongly recommend sturdy footwear!"

On the other hand, Wenthien advises against taking immediate advantage of the opportunity, offered in the Sisyphus prospectus, to spend the night in an authentic slum at the home of a large and typical slum family: "After all, we've just got here. And even on this shady hotel terrace, I can see the climate is getting you down."

Of course Harm and Dörte Peters could land first in Bombay. And, making his first appearance there, Dr. Wenthien, who knows his way around everywhere, could, along with the Parsi temple mentioned in the brochure, recommend another Sisyphus offering, namely, "Camp Cheetah," an enormous waterfront slum. With three other members of the tourist group they visit this far-flung abode of misery (after paying the usual supplement not mentioned in the prospectus). On the way there in a Sisyphus minibus, Dr. Wenthien tells them phase by phase the entire history of the slum, which only a few years earlier was called the Janatha Colony and located near the Nuclear Research Center of India. "Obviously, that wouldn't do. Declared a security risk, the slum was razed by bulldozers. In record time the seventy thousand slum dwellers were moved to Camp Cheetah, an area that is flooded as often as not in the monsoon season. Unfortunately, it's right near the naval arsenal, so again it's a security risk. Human garbage, society's rejects. You see that India, too, has its problems with safeguards."

Dörte's question—Harm later called it naïve—whether housing worthy of human beings had been built in the evacuated Janatha area, almost wrung a laugh from Dr. Wenthien. "Heavens, no! The area is now occupied by a recreation center for the nuclear research people, with swimming pool, golf course, and hall of culture. That's the way it is. You can't stop progress. Even in this country the élites insist on their privileges."

Be that as it may, the two of them could experience their first shock in one or the other slum, in Klong Toei or Camp Cheetah, or a first shock in Bombay and a second (including a night spent in a slum dwelling for an extra charge) in Bangkok. Wherever they land, Dr. Wenthien is already there—as in the race between the hare and the tortoise. After breakfast, when helping the group to settle their program for the day, he speaks German like a native of Hanover. In the gigantic Camp Cheetah slum, he translates their questions into Hindi, and when the largely casteless—that is, untouchable—slum dwellers answer, he displays his mastery of several dialects and of the Tamil spoken in southern India. Thus Dörte and Harm learn

35

that nearly all the children are worm-ridden and that the slum dwellers have to buy their water in jerrycans, because Camp Cheetah is not hooked up to the municipal water supply.

Since Dr. Wenthien has also mastered the language of the Thais, he could, once our couple have become acclimatized, arrange for them to spend a day and a night with a Thai family in the Klong Toei slum. The experiences he purveys are real ones. Things one doesn't forget: the stench of the sewage swamp hovering over the hodgepodge of stilted shacks, the flies, the rats, the cramped quarters, and the hospitality of the cheerful family of twelve, whose neighbors were cutting down on their rations to fatten up a baby for an infant beauty contest organized by a leading daily. Harm is allowed to film the baby with his super 8. Asked how many children they have, the couple try to explain their problem—Yes-to-baby No-to-baby—to their hosts in simple English with gestures. The prolific hosts understand nothing but are amazed.

Unable to sleep, Dörte switches on her flashlight and writes in her diary: "What shocks me most is the cheerfulness of these poverty-stricken people. They always find something to laugh about. Wenthien is a creep but knows his business. Of course what we're doing is cynical. But with the board we are paying—a measly ten marks apiece—the family can scrape along for two weeks. All our democratic consumers ought to spend a night or two in one of these slums. Maybe that would disgust them with our loathsome glut. . . ."

All the same, Harm and Dörte are glad when it's time to get back to the air-conditioned hotel, to a real toilet, a shower, and a refrigerator stocked with drinks. Since they alone of their group have taken advantage of the Sisyphus overnight offer, Dr. Wenthien congratulates them on their "courage and love of reality." True, they hadn't taken any chances. Wenthien had provided them with bottles of germfree hotel water, with antiseptic tablets, biscuits, and cellophane-wrapped fruit. (Some years earlier he had delivered some middle-class German gentlemen thus forearmed to the brothels of Bangkok.)

On this occasion it should be shown—hand reaching into refrigerator on their return from the slum—that Harm has stowed the flown-in, vacuum-sealed liver sausage among beer bottles. And since we mean to shoot our film in an election year, Dr. Wenthien, on their arrival in Bombay or after their night in the slum (or, later, amid Balinese sights), could screw up his face maliciously and ask the two Holsteiners about the would-be chancellor's chances: "I hear you're politically active. So tell me, will this be a first step in the Bavarianization of Germany? Since the Thirty Years' War, as you know, certain accounts between German and German have remained unsettled."

Or we drop India, Thailand, Java, and Bali, and shoot the picture without Dr. Wenthien, in the People's Republic of China, where, if they let us shoot it, native guides will be supplied. But even if the title and the alternance of Yes-to-baby No-to-baby remained the same, this would give us an entirely different film.

No slums in Peking, Shanghai, Kweilin, or Canton. Only Hong Kong shows what the West can do: that God-willed contrast, blessed every Sunday of the year. Wealth crying to high heaven side by side with poverty hidden away in cagelike slums. The right of the stronger to control the market. Hell (and its functionaries) on earth. The world theater as it is today: ragged extras and natty policemen. In the People's Republic of China, this contrast is absent, though the people are not uniformly the same. Streamers featuring Great-granddaddy's motto "Poor but clean" might predominate, were it not for those house-high billboards on which the "four modernizations" provide an alarmingly cheerful illustration of a computer-trusting future lusting for rockets and addicted to growth. They have the Great Leap Forward, the Hundred Flowers, the Cultural Revolution, and the Gang of Four behind them; thrown back, they have retrieved themselves with difficulty, moved mountains, got the better of hunger, liquidated one another, yet increased in numbers, and will soon reach the billion mark without any chance of a matching increase in the acreage devoted to rice, wheat, millet, maize, and soybeans. They show themselves to the West in their present condition and are eager—as every Chinese says with ambivalent politeness—to learn from the West. Actually, we could (should) learn.

But Western arrogance is interested only in (apart from the shops) the ups and downs of Chinese liberalization. What we regard as freedom. Reporters for *Stern* and *Der Spiegel* count girls with skirts, permanented heads, traces of lipstick, and similar attributes of Western liberalism, photograph them, caption them, and let preconceived opinions jell into misinformation. Would it not be more accurate and hence fairer to judge the Chinese nation and its social order by comparison with conditions in those Third World countries that have exposed themselves to Western liberalism as manifested by the Western economic system, and whose dismal achievements are known as flight from the land, slums, overcropping, erosion, undernourishment and starvation, luxury and misery, lawless tyranny, and, towering over them all, corruption?

If our teacher couple from Itzehoe on the Stör are (in the film as in reality) to travel to China, they should previously have smelled the great Indian slums, seen the starving northeast of Thailand, gained some idea of Indonesian corruption, and everywhere recognized the destructive power and effective curse of the Western economic system as exacerbated by Japan: the tyranny of the free market, progress at any price, Swiss numbered accounts for fugitive capital, increasing poverty.

Naturally Dörte and Harm Peters, who even in China wouldn't know whether or not to bring a child into the world, would be only too ready in India, Thailand, and Indonesia to confirm their prior knowledge by using the word neocolonialism. ("Look at that!" cries Harm. "They've got a finger in every pie. Siemens and Unilever . . .") Besides, Indian fatalism, Javanese gentleness, and the happy-go-lucky laughter of the Thais provide semblances of an explanation that one can travel with. ("My God!" cries Dörte. "The way these people just live from day to day; none of our obsession with security!") But the governments of all three countries are sovereign. They rule neither fatalistically nor gently, and certainly not happy-go-luckily from day to day, but with military and police power, with caste arrogance and corruption, with all the instruments of power inherited from the native past or donated delivery-free by Western arsenals.

"Oh, well," says Dörte Peters. "It wouldn't be fair to judge conditions here by our democratic ideas."

"That's a fact," says Harm Peters. "Even Mao wouldn't have got anywhere with Hinduism."

He is interested in social problems, he wants to know everyone's hourly and weekly wage; she wants to store up schoolworthy facts in her diary. Both say, "Before we demand freedom of speech here, we should do something about our own. . . ."

Some of their fellow travelers were of the same opinion. And Dr. Wenthien, who tends to air his world view every evening over a glass of orange juice, instructs his small and by this time mildly exasperated travel group: "Unfortunate and in need of Western help as these people

39

may seem, this is where the future of our planet will be decided. These are the people who will impose the new human rights on us Westerners, who can't stop shooting off our mouths about human rights. Europe's hunger for the secrets of Asia, I can assure you, will be stilled for all time. All their demons and spirits—and believe me, they exist—will descend on us."

Wenthien utters these words as the group, by common consent, are about to spend their last day on Indian soil near a fishing village outside of Bombay. This is supposed to be restful, and, sure enough, the day begins in an atmosphere of rural peace. An old-fashioned ferry, worthy of being much photographed, carries them to the island of Manori. Loaded into oxcarts, they photograph the road to their simple but clean resthouse over the magnificent horns of the draft animals.

"At last, no air conditioning!" cries Dörte.

"At last, the sea!" cries Harm.

And palms that can be photographed heavenward. And a wide sandy beach where a stranded turtle becomes a photograph. And native women who serve young coconuts and tea. They have knotted their saris between their legs; but Harm hesitates to photograph their striking gait. On the way along the beach to the fishing village—"But kindly keep your clothes on!" Dr. Wenthien pleads—Dörte, suddenly persuaded by nature, the palms, and the strangely knotted women—"All this, somehow it turns me on!"—wants a baby after all: "Our child, hear? We've got to want it, not just think about it. Want it with our guts, not just our heads. With an animal urge, d'you hear?"

But Harm, who admits that all this—"It, you know, the magic spell"—turns him on, too, is unwilling to send his head on vacation. "Assuming," he says, "we have a baby. Assuming it's born healthy. Assuming even that it grows up without the usual childhood traumas. And assuming that, insofar as our professional lives permit, we really look after this planned child. Even then, it'll go wrong. I tell you, the environment, our school system, the TV compulsion, everything, everything, I tell you, will warp and standardize our child. Same as we've been warped and standardized. And think of the new technologies! Suppose our child is plugged into the school computer. Not by himself, of course; the whole class, the whole school-age population. Beginning, say, in the late eighties, our old-fashioned human teachers—much too costly and hard to control—will be phased out, replaced by government-programmed teaching computers: knowledge will be shot straight into our little darlings' brain cells—bzz, bzzz! No more of your stupid cramming. The multiplication table? Injected in half an hour. Bzzz. English irregular verbs? Ten minutes. Bzzz! Vocabulary lists? Don't make me laugh. The child's handy bedroom computer will take care of all that. And with all those dates, figures, formulas, verbs stored up in their brains, the little dears will know everything and nothing. And we, Mother Dörte, Father Harm, will stand there like fools, with nothing in our heads but superfluous memories, imprecise knowledge, and moral scruples. Are you, I ask you, going to take responsibility for such a child?"

Already, propelled by Harm's speech, they're in the center of the village, if this village has a center. Tumbledown shacks, clay huts. What the nets bring in, finger-long fishes and still smaller fry, are drying on hard floors and wall-high rows of stakes. Neither boats nor nets nor fish nor the mill where the fish is ground up into fish meal belongs to the fishermen. The village is said to number five thousand inhabitants, three thousand of them children. Worm-ridden, visibly ill, marked by eye diseases. They don't beg, they don't laugh or play; they're just quietly too many.

41

On the way back, Dörte, who only a short while be-fore had been turned on by so much nature and longed with an animal urge for a child, says, "The slum kids were more fun." In the evening, on the terrace of the modest resthouse, Dr. Wenthien lectures his little group about the Indian fishing industry: "It doesn't pay off. And yet the Indian Ocean, except for the fished-out coastal waters, is teeming with fish; if deep-sea fishing were developed, it would relieve the protein deficiency of the predominantly vegetarian population in the coastal regions, and far into the interior if deepfreeze storage chains were set up. But the Indians—oh, well. All they can do is multiply. Fifty-seven thousand babies a day. Every month a million more Indians. The Chinese ought to introduce *their* order."

That night, under the mosquito netting, when Dörte comes back to the child and cites Wenthien's exemplary Chinese ("They actually encourage one-child marriages in the People's Republic"), Harm shouts, "No! No! The Germans can die out for all I care."

Would that be so bad? Think of all the great culture-bearing nations that can be admired only in museums today! The Hittites, the Sumerians, the Aztecs! Isn't it conceivable that in a thousand years the children of a rising new nation will stand gazing at glass cases, marveling at the housing arrangements and eating habits of the Germans? At their unswerving industry? At their tendency to classify everything, even their dreams? And mightn't the German language become, as the Latin of the Romans has today, a dead language, though still quotable? And in a thousand years or so, mightn't politicians, who at present ornament their bank-overflowing speeches with Latin maxims, spice their logorrhea with quotations from Höl-derlin: "And so I went among the Germans . . . I cannot conceive of a nation more divided . . ."? And is it not possible that German culture (and with it literature) will come to be prized as an indivisible but manifold unity only after and because the Germans have become extinct? "No," someone may say in retrospect, "they were not mere warlike barbarians, concerned only with sordid gain, mere function without spirit. . . ."

I'm writing through my hat. Wherever we stopped, I loyally wrote "writer" on the "profession" line of my immigration card. A profession with a long tradition, if the word was really in the beginning. A fine, dangerous, presumptuous, dubious profession that invites metaphoric epithets. An East German apparatchik, a Chinese Red Guard, or Goebbels in his day might have said what Franz Josef Strauss, leaving his Latin on the shelf, said a year ago in German. Writers, he said, were "rats and blowflies." (Later there was some argument as to whether he and those who took up his phrase had meant not all but only some writers.)

Even though his name was not uttered in China, it was of him we were speaking whenever the conversation turned to a certain comparable worldwide usage. Chinese writers are familiar with the contemptible power that likens its enemies to rodents and insects and is only too ready to exterminate them. They spoke rather diffidently, as though exposing their own disgrace, of their sufferings during the bad years: imprisoned, flogged, forbidden to write, put on public display, condemned to latrine duty. That was over, but its effects lingered on. For which reason the new literature, still halting and formally poor, was known as "wounded literature."

They asked about East German colleagues. (An elderly member of the Peking Circle had spoken with Anna Seghers at a congress years before.) I told them how we had met regularly—four or five West Berlin writers, seven or eight East Berlin writers—from 1973 to 1977 in an assortment of East Berlin apartments, read to one another from our manuscripts, deplored our fragmented situation and glorified our nevertheless still-common language. I said: "About every three months. Yes, over beer and potato salad. The host's wife would pull the names of the readers out of a hat as though drawing lots. Of course we were spied on. We kept it up as long as we could. Then the expatriation began. It started with Biermann."

I named the names and book titles of those writers who are now residing in the West, yet seem to be living between the two states, a thorn in the flesh of both Germanys. And in Shanghai, where I was again sitting among colleagues, they, too, attached importance to every detail: the border control, the underhanded methods of the censors, their Eastern-Western way of treating writers. Everything connected with us restlessly sedentary nest-befoulers.

It didn't seem foreign or too far afield. Chinese writers know all about ideological blindness and dogmatic blinkers. The contempt with which the mighty express themselves is graven on their minds. Only the words "rats and blowflies" had to be translated for them, not the extermination implied. They said: "Even our classics were demolished. Now we are having to rediscover them for our young people, who know very little."

Sitting in a formal, at first ceremonial circle, we conversed. After-dinner speeches were not avoided. (I would have liked to read poems by Kunert and Born.) We ate with chopsticks—sweet-and-sour sea cucumbers, Peking duck, and jellied century-old eggs. We drank 120-proof millet spirits. What did we drink to? Since our glasses were often refilled, we drank to contradictions, to the repeatedly contested truth, naturally to the health of the people (whoever they may be), and to the white, still-spotless

44

paper that clamors to be spotted with words. And we drank to ourselves, the rats and blowflies.

Among my slips for *Headbirths* a parenthetical note reads: "(Before the teacher couple set out, or after they return to Itzehoe at the end of August, Dörte Peters says, 'Not yet, Harm. We'll have to wait for the election returns. I will not bring a child into the world under Strauss.')" Simply ridiculous. This pretext must be pulled out from under her.

4

Nicolas Born has been dying for weeks. We visit him at the Westend Clinic in Berlin. Generalized cancer. After the removal of one lung and a brain operation, his Westphalian skull (now shaved and shrunken) is more or less at rest. The doctors give him three months.

He apologizes for his condition. We, in good health, are sitting beside his bed. Just as I'm going to tell him about the Döblin Prize being awarded to Gerold Späth, he asks us not to require names and events of his memory. It has sprung holes, he says. Words missing, too. He lies restlessly on his back, searching the ceiling for lost subordinate clauses. Irmgard Born cranks up the head section of the bed. Lying on his side makes the constant pain more endurable.

"Say, where have you all . . ." We try to speak normally and not as though taking leave. We tell him things that his head needn't remember—about the Chinese bicycle riders, about two Chinese sailors Ute noticed in Shanghai, walking tenderly hand in hand, a couple. The image makes him smile. (Or is he only trying to give us pleasure by acknowledging something that's supposed to cheer him up?) Then he feels tired but he can't sleep—all the many many medicines.

(Now I'm reading his book *False Witness* [*Die Fälschung*], which he finished with his last remaining strength. It reads like an anticipation of his, our sickness— the absurdity of the normal. Accidents that have ceased to frighten us. The exploitation of horror. The sophistries of madness. The closeness that alienates. Love, that will-o'- the-wisp. The narrowing of our condition.) Strange that he, childlike like most writers, should be waiting almost defiantly for the forthcoming review of his book in *Der Spiegel*. When, he wants to know, will it be Monday?

No sooner have we left our friend—abandoned him, actually—no sooner is the Westend Clinic behind us, than everything that no longer concerns him is there again: the corner café (we—we!—need a pick-me-up), the traffic, the future and its aims, the scheduling of the next few hours and days, school and tax problems, the weather, the coming menace, which, *faute de mieux*, can go by the name of Strauss, and more distant threats—Khomeini. But there's also a taxi that can be called, cigarettes, small change, the backwash of our trip to Asia. How was it? Tell us. That's what I'm doing: Headbirths.

In my notes I read: "On the beach in Bali as on the Indian island of Manori, Harm Peters picks up sea shells, which, though Dörte doesn't care for them, he wants to display, along with some shells found on European beaches, in their home in Itzehoe: on window sills, in a vitrine, or in old-fashioned candy jars."

A man on a beach, walking and repeatedly bending down. He has run away from her and her problems. Now that she wants a child—"This time my mind is made up!" —she has been tiptoeing on religious pathways. With Bali-

48

nese women she offers up little flower-patterned bowls of rice in temples under holy trees, in each of which a white, fertility-bestowing woman is said to dwell. Dr. Wenthien, who is familiar with their—hers and Harm's—problem, has advised her in words drawn from his stock of Hindu lore: "Rather than dismiss our desires as the work of evil spirits, we should give them pure expression."

For that reason she has stopped sleeping with Harm. "Not yet," she says. "I haven't got to that stage yet." Morosely Harm paces the beach. Near him some old women are dragging dripping baskets full of shell splinters through the surf for a beggarly wage. The splinters are ground up by mill owners and burned to lime by furnace owners. Harm shouts into the surf: "That's what you think, baby! But it won't work. When you finally want it, I won't want it. This temple shit! I don't want an irrational child!"

Then he helps an old woman—who thinks it's funny —carry her shell splinters. Rather awkwardly he heaves her basket.

While still in Bombay, and later in Bangkok, Dörte Peters has looked for Hindu knickknacks between visits to temples and slums, and in junk shops come across the child god, the thumb-size dancing Siva of the childhood phase on his little pedestal. But not until she gets to Bali, which, quite unlike the other thirteen thousand Indonesian islands, displays itself daily to its tourists in accordance with Hindu rites, does this rather sober-minded and undoubtedly fact-obsessed schoolteacher swing to the supernatural; as Harm says, "she's on a religious trip."

Maybe it's the sky-reflecting water of the terraced rice paddies, the bamboo groves, the cloud-shrouded volcano, the threatened, blessed landscapes changing at every turn in the road, the waringin trees spreading their shady roofs

49

over the center of every village, that make Dörte religious and hence receptive. Though unable to adapt herself to their gliding gait, she walks in a row with the Balinese women, carrying in her hands what they carry piled on their heads, and hangs (after presenting her rice offering) her wishing slip on a wishing tree that promises offspring. Now her slip is flowering among many slips, all asking for a child, another child in addition to the many others; whereas Dörte has in mind her first and (she has no doubt) only child.

"Whoever thou art, good spirit," she has written on her wishing slip and, with elaborate explanations, in her diary, "bless me with a daughter. Her name shall be Lambon." (She has got this name from a novel Wenthien lent her: *Love and Death on Bali*.) The daughter of the peasant Hinrich Wulf writes in her diary: "If the outlandish name makes Father angry—What kind of a name is that! he will fume—I'll ask him why they called me Dörte."

She already knows the rites and observes the taboos. To prove the purity of her wish, she has thrown her pills, three packs, into a cave, recommended to the group by Dr. Wenthien, naturally a holy or demonic one inhabited by a snake goddess and termed "Cave of Bats" in the Sisyphus brochure. Harm will snap her doing it or film the happening with his super 8.

Before this episode jells into a movie sequence, I should add that Harm has tried several times to deliver his flown-in liver sausage. So far in vain. In Denpasar, the capital city of the island, where he looks for his school friend, showing his address to all and sundry, Uwe Jensen is not to be found. Every time Harm, sweating, carrying the liver sausage in a shopping bag, shows his slip of paper, he is sent in a different direction. Unintelligible floods of words. Offers to buy. Tips to invariably cheerful young fellows, who guide him to remote shantytowns. Plenty of untouristic reality. And that in the noonday heat, while Dörte lies in the shade, under hotel palms. Even for a vacuum-sealed liver sausage, this is too much. Goes against its nature. It wants to get back to the Kuta Beach Hotel. It wants to lie safe in the refrigerator.

After another search scene—this time at city police headquarters, but without the sausage in the shopping bag —Harm will appeal for help to Dr. Wenthien, who of course knows what to do. Through personal contacts he introduces the not undangerous subplot, which the liver sausage has promised from the start: complications, forged bills of lading, Chinese commission agents, a Malay kris....

I don't like it. The vanished Uwe Jensen could be mixed up in arms deals, which in line with Ambler's plot tendencies and Harm Peters's love of adventure, could develop into the main plot. Wenthien's hints—"Your friend," he says, "is presumably visiting the island of Timor on business"—suggest arms smuggling; because in East Timor, formerly a Portuguese colony, an independence movement is still fighting the Indonesian military, and Timor, like Bali, is one of the Lesser Sunda Islands.

No, we won't get mixed up in that. At the most such a subplot might be hinted at as a headbirth directed against Dörte's planned child. As *his* plan. In daydreams Harm sees himself as a partisan. Firing away with a (Russian) Tommy gun. In a tropical rain forest, in the mountains. Providing covering fire. Fighting side by side with his friend Uwe for a free and independent Timor. Risking their lives, because it's too late to delete the liver sausage from the script.

But the plot-fostering sausage might be counterbalanced by various natural miracles. On my slips it says,

51

"Outside the Cave of Bats, in whose church-door-high entrance and deep-vaulted darkness hang a hundred thousand bats, Harm and Dörte quarrel."

About the child, of course. A shrill squeak, crescendo decrescendo, emanates from the bats. The cave breathes what a film can't communicate: stink. Three, four dozen of the hundred thousand bats break loose, dart about in zigzags, and hang themselves up again, head down, in the vault. The little temple in the cave entrance is encrusted with bat droppings. The immeasurable blackness of the cave is supposed to contain a snake, or a goddess in snake form. Some little girls among the beggar children, who have followed Wenthien and his tourist group, hold out baskets of flowers. Dörte buys one and sets it down in front of the shit-encrusted temple.

Ignoring the group, Harm shouts: "If I make a child, I want to do it consciously. Do you hear? Not the Hindu way!"

And Dörte shouts shamelessly: "I can't make it with our shitty reason! I have to break free, to let go. I need something different, the force that comes from inside, no, from outside, all right, laugh, something supersensory, a divine power, whatever...."

Now she rummages in her pocket. Now at last, with a fine sweeping movement, she throws the three packs of pills into the cave, and then she runs, as though forced to follow the pills, past the little temple and disappears into the cave, her light-colored dress and long blond hair swallowed up by the dark hole.

The tourist group utters low-to-shrill screams of horror. Even Dr. Wenthien grants his face a look of rigid terror. Harm yells and curses, then raises his super 8 and films, as if that could help, the bat-traversed blackness until he sees his Dörte coming back in the viewfinder.

She is moving slowly. Step by step her color lightens.

She smiles. She has a bat in her hair. She stands facing the still-filming Harm and the cowering tourist group. She smiles as she never smiled before. She disentangles the bat from her hair, and the bat flits away. The now silent beggar children touch her hands, her sandaled feet; they try to take hold of her blond hair, which is now blonder still. Obviously happy, Dörte weeps.

Rather embarrassed, the group turn away. (We hear Dr. Wenthien whispering, among other foreign words, the word *karma*.) A mongrel that was lying asleep in the cave entrance gets up and eats a dead bat that fell off the vault. Harm shouts, "No! I want to go home!"

In my notes, the question is asked: "Will she, after this scene, still be unwilling to sleep with him? Or can it be that she, at last pure enough, wants to, but that he wants to no longer, because he now has to, or thinks he has to? Or that he can't, though he now has leave to and also wants to?"

I think he'll refuse. After all, he (like Dörte, for that matter) belongs to a generation that ten years earlier committed itself to the principle of refusal: resolved to throw off all sexual and social constraints. To be guided exclusively by the pleasure principle. True, very little of that is left, for in the meantime they have found themselves knee-deep in prosperity-determined consumption and pleasureless sex, but the student protest phase left sufficient imprint to keep the words and concepts of their early years available to them as an alternative, as something they can relapse into wherever they may be sitting or lying.

In their hotel room, looking out at the balcony which Dörte, as Harm puts it, "has converted into a home temple," he has this certainty: "It's your flight into religious patterns that keeps my cock down."

Even if he wanted to, he can't. Her at first submissive, then frankly aggressive expectancy drives him, he says, "into a disgustingly subservient role." When, half enticing, half threatening, she says, "Oh, come on, Harm. I'll get it up for you," he builds word barriers: "I suppose I have to do my stint. Forced labor, I call it. Having to when I neither can nor want to—if that isn't alienation, I ask you, what is? And all on account of a religious mania. What has that got to do with me? You can get that from someone else. Well, from your confessor, your sky pilot!"

The tourist group to whom Dr. Wenthien explains the religious rites of the Parsis in Bombay, the begging techniques of the Buddhist monks in Bangkok, the subliminal Hinduism in Javanese Islam, and on Bali the Hinduism that has kept its childlike character in spite of Dutch punitive expeditions, consists of two couples in their mid-forties, two girl friends in their late thirties, a statuesque mother with a sickly daughter, a pastor's merry widow, a retired tax official from Wilhelmshaven, and Harm and Dörte Peters. Or we could throw in another couple in their mid-forties and subtract the pastor's widow. In any case, the members of the group avail themselves in varying degree of the attractions offered by Sisyphus. One of the couples abstains from visiting slums. The statuesque mother's sickly daughter has seen enough temples. Only Harm and Dörte are interested in spending a night in the slum. The Cave of Bats is shunned by the girl friends in their late thirties and the tax official from Wilhelmshaven, who, on the other hand, waxes indignant—"Always wanting to be original!"—when Harm and Dörte break away from the group ("Sick of plodding around with the horde!") and go off on perilous excursions of their own.

The whole group comes into the picture only in the morning when discussing the day's program with Dr.

Wenthien in the hotel lobby, on brief fade-ins of excursions in the air-conditioned VW bus, during the boat ride on the khlongs of Bangkok, or in pan shots of the cockfight, which, by the way, is forbidden by law. Still, the uncontrollable betting passion of the Balinese puts it within the realm of the possible, and Wenthien's connections enable the tourist group to attend.

Under a translucent roof of palm leaves. On a village square. Sudden silence after a long palaver. During the very first fight scene Wenthien finds occasion for a lengthy speech, which, in line with his profession, he must already have made a number of times. "See those knife blades on the spurs? The way they leap at each other! And pounce! And now watch those stupid cocks, how the moment they lose sight of each other, they stop puffing themselves up and set about pecking at grains in peaceful boredom. Just like people, who need incitement before they'll fight each other, but it can happen anywhere, on the shop floor, in democratic assemblies, in the marriage bed if need be. Just think of our battles over wage scales, of the new divorce law, or the present election campaign: those puffed-up political fighting cocks. . . ."

This he says in a rather whining undertone, as though bored by his own wisdom, under the light-filtering palm-leaf roof, surrounded by his tourist group, in the midst of Balinese men, who were gentle only a moment ago but are now shaken by the gaming passion. How they squat there. How the sweat marks their muscles. How they fight one another with finger signs and guttural sounds. How the men breathe on their fighting cocks, kiss them, blow on their feathers, fondle them.

Women are not admitted when the fighting cocks leap at each other with knife blades on their spurs; only tourist women are admitted. Defeated cocks are butchered on the edge of the ring. Dörte's upper lip is perspiring. The sickly daughter wants to leave: "Can't stand any more of this." The girls in their late thirties take pictures. "What exposure?" cries the tax official from Wilhelmshaven. Someone else is enthusiastic. "Man, see those feathers fly!" And Harm with his super 8 films long and meticulously.

He wants to show—his wish and his anticipation of its fulfillment can be faded in—his local SPD section the irrationality yet social relevance of Balinese cockfighting. "That, dear comrades and parimutuel fans, is the traditional method of rule by bread and circuses." And Dörte is drawn in. "Hold the light meter, will you?"

"You see," says Dr. Wenthien, "when the cocks get listless, the handlers perform a little ritual and put baskets over them. That revives their fighting spirit. Once the baskets are lifted off with the appropriate ritual, you can be sure the fight will go on."

"Like the comrades in Itzehoe!" cries Harm, while filming with enthusiasm. "As soon as some sacred principle is brought in."

Two fresh cocks are put in the ring. They puff themselves up. Off to the side, the butcher is getting to work. "Don't look, child!" says the statuesque mother to her sickly daughter. The cock's armed foot is chopped off and put aside, so the knife blade can be sharpened for other fights, for other cocks. Dörte hisses, "Men! Men! Only a man could think of such a thing!" The girls in their late thirties think it's all "too-too picturesque." The tax official has trouble inserting a new roll of film. "Can't somebody help me?" And over it all Dr. Wenthien whines sagely: "The eternal return. Everything flows. Die and be born...." Cut.

Whereupon the always unchanged and seemingly sexless tour guide, standing (but without his tourist group and without Harm Peters) beside a Hindu temple, looks past Dörte Peters in the direction of the sea and surf and says insistently and hypnotically: "Therefore you must not seek to evade the cycle, but humbly enter into it, conceive, carry and bear a child in order that the eternal die-and-be-born . . . So tomorrow we shall visit the Cave of Bats, where a hundred thousand bats are hanging head down. . . ."

This much is clear: we won't shoot the picture in China, even if Schlöni, as our children call him, gets permission. In the People's Republic they've eliminated starvation, made dying a little less compulsive, and by an enormous effort (though too late) brought the urge to be born under control. Only the first child is subsidized. When a second child is born, the subsidy for the first is withdrawn. If Chinese parents dare to bring a third child into the world, they have to repay all sums received for the first.

But that, Harm Peters might say, is inhuman, cruel, constrictive, frustrating! And no premarital sex. And no extramarital sex. What on earth do they do with their emotions, yearnings, surplus energy, their reproductive urge, and their innate desire for a large family?

In other words: What sort of complexes set in? What kind of neuroses? Have the Chinese even got time for complexes, neuroses, and suchlike Western fads? And supposing they have a neurosis or two, where can they go with them? Should the Western world—always so glad to help—gratify the Chinese nation with five hundred thousand psychiatrists? Would this be a useful way of getting rid of our brain surplus? Would this be that other film, which Schlöndorff and I don't have to make? And if we Germans instead of the Chinese had hit the billion mark, would we, because we had been deprived of all pre- and extramarital pleasure, have to live with the unrecognizable, on-no-couch-analyzed complexes and neuroses of the Chinese, while in our stead the Chinese nation, shrunken to eighty and even fewer million, threatened with extinction and supersaturated with pleasure, would be tormented by our German-type complexes and neuroses and consequently obliged to feed an increasing number of psychiatrists, psychoanalysts, and psychotherapists?

I forgot to ask whether psychoanalysis exists in the People's Republic of China. Whether anyone has time and money for that long-drawn-out ritual. Whether possibly some different kind of libidinal satisfaction ... Or whether, perhaps, why not, with the help of acupuncture ...

Soon after the abortion two years ago, Dörte and Harm Peters, because of their Yes-to-baby No-to-baby, went into analysis, separately and together. Nothing much came to light: Harm's medium-sized mother complex and Dörte's excessive father fixation. Much as they liked to disagree, they both found the weekly two-hour session too expensive. "I already know, without having to pay for it, that I still have a childish fondness for my ma. So let's take a trip instead."

"Maybe the trip will help us develop," said Dörte. "Because I intend to keep my attachment for my father, even if the old curmudgeon does get on my nerves now and then with his prehistoric experiences in Siberia."

This can be brought into the picture: the frail (soldier's) widow in her one-family house, the landless peasants of the region. And Harm and Dörte on the couch, not a double, always a single couch. The mummymumblings. The quarrels with Father. The last and next-to-last dreams unfolded, the imprintings of the first anal phase chewed over while Harm's mother in Hademarschen and Dörte's

58

father in his apartment in Krempe are unaware of their son-and-daughter-imprinting power, but enjoy their son's attentions (goodies from Kruse's Delicatessen) and their stimulating arguments with their daughter (the farm they sold for a song). (Dörte's mother, though she still washes the dishes, is mentioned only in passing.)

If this flashback is necessary, the psychoanalyst, as far as I'm concerned, could look like Dr. Wenthien and whine sagely with Wenthien's voice, "If your objective desire for a child conflicts with your subjective fear of a child, resulting by turns in refusal of sex and loss of potency, then your mother complex, then your father fixation . . ."

But it needn't be. Wenthien needn't play a double role in our movie. Or only if he is conceivable in still other roles: Indian guru, Balinese village priest.

For instance, he could send our couple from the Kuta Beach Hotel on a rented scooter into the paradisiacal interior of Bali. And there, under the waringin tree that shades a village square, Harm and Dörte meet an old, or ageless, man who, though squatting in a Balinese loincloth, is played by the same actor—Schlöni suggests Otto Sander —as Dr. Wenthien, the tour guide and Itzehoe psychoanalyst.

For they are all interchangeable. Our complexes and neuroses are mass-produced articles. Wenthien could teach group dynamics or work in a mail-order house. There are teachers like Harm and Dörte in every district capital. And Itzehoe with its modernization damage, its garbage-disposal problem and pedestrian zone, might just as well be called Tuttlingen and be situated on some other river.

Only Brokdorf is Brokdorf. How this Brokdorf, town, parish, and holiday resort, has been mollified with a swimming pool and bludgeoned with a walled-in nuclear construction site that is growing more and more idyllic, how it lies directly behind the Elbe dike, waiting for a prince to come, wake it with a kiss, and countermand the court order that has brought construction to a standstill—only in the German fairy-tale literature do such things happen. So there our Sleeping Beauty waits, ringed around by barbed wire. An ideal spot for demonstrations and police action. Five years ago Harm and Dörte came here to protest. Here they might almost have brought themselves to use force. Now and then they come here to be rejuvenated. They still like to talk about it: "Remember the cops, up here and down there, the way we . . ." This is their place.

Looking across the fenced-off zone from the dike, the eye sees far into the cattle-rich Wilstermarsch. The world-embracing gaze spreads from the dike across the Elbe beach, broad at low tide, and across the Elbe, which, widening as it approaches the nearby estuary, carries giant tankers, banana boats, and coastal steamers to and from Hamburg. And, hungry for distance, the gaze sweeps still farther, beyond the far shore, out yonder where Lower Saxony, as flat as the marshland on this side, begins. Ah, and the cloud formations over so much flatland. And the inky sunsets. A feast for the camera!

And, unmoved by the halted, still-threatening construction project—for on November 26 the Schleswig court will be in session again—calves graze, sheep keep the dike grass short, the wind shifts, season follows season, nature plays dumb.

From here we, the film, must keep making a fresh start, for we, the film, keep falling back on Brokdorf, that headbirth. Who would deny us permission to film here? What other vanishing point would our teachers have then?

Dörte Peters is absolutely opposed on existential grounds—"It's a crime against nature, against people!" She trots out arguments that are always "somehow": "Then we must somehow economize or somehow find other sources of energy." In the interest of the workers—"After all, they're the ones who always have to pay!"—Harm is in favor, but with reservations. "Naturally, they first have to find solutions to the problem of safeguards, and specifically, medium- and long-term means of waste disposal. Otherwise it's no go."

Dörte and Harm have taken positions. Her "somehow against," his "for with reservations" travel through Asia with them, along with his vacuum-sealed liver sausage, natural casing and all, and along with their transportable quarrel over the child, whose existence, questionable from the start, has come to depend more and more on the nuclear energy question: "One more fast breeder and our child has had it, as far as I'm concerned."

This Dörte Peters says, not on the Elbe dike at Brokdorf, but shortly before her religious visitation in Bombay, where Harm, soon after their visit to the slum in the former Janatha Colony now named Camp Cheetah, is stricken with diarrhea, because he has taken his enterovioform too late.

Without the group (or Wenthien), they are looking for souvenirs. And in the midst of the street crowd, possibly within view of the Nuclear Research Center, which is situated on a slight rise in the ground, he shits in his pants. Beggars and children, in whose eyes nothing could be more natural, swarm around him as it drips through the light tropical cotton. Dörte is embarrassed. Harm shouts: "Who cares! Here everybody shits where he pleases!"

Childishly exuberant (or should one say: happily freed from his inhibitions) he hops about in his shitty trousers. Now, at last, he belongs. Foreign no longer. He has a new, absolutely new sense of freedom. No more ontheonehand-ontheother. "At last!" Harm shouts. "Man, does this feel good!" He squats by the roadside among other squatters. A squatter hands him a betel nut. He chews the betel nut and will spit red juice like other squatters.

Sweating and shivering, Dörte stands in the midst of them, then off to one side. She doesn't belong, she smells foreign. Her blue-and-white-striped summer dress is spotless. She keeps on being blond, too blond, exaggeratedly, overwhelmingly blond, fundamentally blond, whereas Harm's ash-blondness darkens, turns blue-black, native-black. And in other ways as well he begins to squalify at the edges, soon becoming unrecognizable, then untouchable, one of those untouchables who, as the statistics tell us, number over eighty million in India.

Dörte weeps, screams, runs away blindly, pursued by begging, scabby, crippled children. Nevertheless, she gets back to the hotel, and there in the cool lobby her Harm, clad in fresh tropical cotton and once more as blond as Dörte, takes her in his arms.

I'd like to discuss that with Born: the preparation for and presentation of horror, the art of bringing it out. But Nicolas Born isn't talking to us any more. He is dying indescribably. Concentrating entirely on himself. As usual —that's how we've always known him—but without communication from his dwindling ego. Never again will he unload in batches. No more long-lined poems. Never again troubled about the right word, though he knows the word that troubles him is the right one. Who else could be so vaguely precise?

For four years we and the others (the Haufs, Meckel, Buch, Peter Schneider) took the train every few months from the Zoo to Friedrichstrasse. With our dissimulated manuscripts, we'd inch our way through the passport and customs inspections. Finally reassembled on the other side, we'd take a cab out to the Schädlichs' on Rotkäppchenweg or the Kunerts' at Berlin-Buch, to Sibylle Hentschke's one-room pad on Lenbachstrasse or to Sarah Kirsch's place in the high-rise building with the fine view from overthere to overthere.

Born was always with us. He'd read from his *The Dark Side*; Schädlich would read his self-excluding, self-encircling stories, Buch the evidence to his dissipated talents, Sarah her tear-raising poems, Kunert prognostications of the impending Ice Age, I samples from my swelling *Flounder*, and Brasch from his concentrated rage. When we weren't reading we talked our necks away. Bugs may have lurked under wallpaper, embedded in plaster. Or possibly there was a spy among us, eating sausages and crumb cake, spooning up cabbage soup with us. The secret police may have heard it all, taken it down from tape, yet learned no more about literature than their colleagues in the West, to whom they may have turned for help in deciphering our writings. What do they understand in East and West about Sarah's line breaks, Kunert's ramblings in cemeteries, or Born's perplexities about words? Behind every semicolon they scent danger. They fear the silence between stanzas. In East as well as West they are certain that when in an intricate context windfall fruit is mentioned (quite incidentally), it's a dig at them.

Toward the end of our meetings—it must have been early in '77, Biermann had already been expatriated, the Schädlichs, Sarah, Brasch, and Jurek Becker were soon to follow—Nicolas Born read the not yet definitive beginning of his *False Witness*. We had no idea, but he may have suspected what was coming.

Now we live dispersed, and rarely phone. We attempted further meetings, but under the altered circumstances they were failures. Since we were all in the West it was hard to listen so intensely. Too much interference.

Yet I know you'd like to read us your rough drafts,

and I'd like to read us mine: vulnerable and self-assured. Schädlich, what makes him so glum. Sarah, how her love lives from one little bone to the next. Jurek, what plagues him. I about headbirths and why the Germans are dying out.

We could talk about the form that has become content: how flash forward and flashback cancel each other out so that everything becomes present. When Dörte and Harm Peters let their childhood memories of the stuffy fifties trickle into their student protest—"Remember when the Student Union . . ."—and drag their veterans' chitchat into the present from Kiel and Neumünster via Itzehoe to the isle of Bali. Or when the two of them, still chewing over the attempt to murder Rudi Dutschke,* foresee themselves in situations that are as good as certain: his illuminating lectures about the Third World, her determination, if Schmidt and Genscher† don't give up their idiotic commitment to nuclear energy, to vote for the environmentalists after all: "Helping Strauss? Maybe, but we've got to risk it."

Or I ask you all—you in particular, Nicolas—whether this damned liver sausage, which has become increasingly real to me, should stay home or be flown to Asia with all the subplots it entails? Mightn't this slowly spoiling foreign body be Harm's passport to trouble?

He already arouses suspicion while asking for his friend's address at the Denpasar police station. Wenthien puts him (and sausage) through via several go-betweens (Chinese, of course) without its dawning on Harm that he

---

* During Easter week 1968, a youth named Bachmann, an admirer of Hitler, shot and critically wounded Rudi Dutschke, the leader of a militant Berlin student group. —Ed.
† Hans-Dietrich Genscher, Minister of Foreign Affairs in the coalition government headed by Chancellor Helmut Schmidt. —Ed.

is getting mixed up in arms smuggling. He even books a charter flight to Timor for himself (and various crates that have been foisted on him as luggage). But does he land among the insurgents? And what has Dörte to say about all this? Or is he arrested before even leaving the Denpasar airport, and questioned? In the course of his interrogation, should the liver sausage be cut open lengthwise, or should only a sample be taken, after which the cut in the vacuum packaging could be patched up with Dermicel. And from a purely practical point of view: can a German liver sausage take all that punishment? Will Wenthien—before we can get back to Yes-to-baby No-to-baby—have to intervene as Harm's guardian angel and rescue him from the clutches of the police?

But never again will Nicolas Born relieve my misgivings with his. Never again will our fictions yield themselves to comparisons. What puts me into a sweat leaves him cold. Ten years younger than I, he never followed a squad leader, never fell out to swear allegiance to the flag; my speculations, offshoots of guilt and complicity, are not his fears; for if, in the midst of my headbirths, I date myself back by ten years, changing my birth date to 1917, he is not with me in the spring of 1941 when I parachute down (along with Max Schmeling) on Crete and live through all the rest of it (without him), writing, intent on words. And it's not only poems in honor of the Führer's birthdays and hymns to Doric columns that come to mind, but also the executions of partisans (which reduce me to silence) and the liquidation of a Ukrainian village that I see in front of me huddled in the snow, just before we smoke it out as ordered. . . .

"What has that got to do with us?" Harm shouts at his Dörte. "We were born after that shit. We're guilty of entirely different shit. But wherever we go they ask us if there are Nazis in Germany again. As if the whole world wished there were. No! We have other worries. Not that everlasting prehistoric stuff. But what's going to happen tomorrow. How we're going to get through the eighties. Even without Strauss. That one's another relic of the day before yesterday. Still trying to hold Stalingrad."

5

Those eighties that are said to lie before us—they've already begun when Harm and Dörte start on their trip. I'm writing in November 1979 and hope to finish the first draft on New Year's Eve, shortly before our guests arrive to share the fish and meat.

Soon Orwell's decade will dawn for us. "No, dear George," another book might begin, "it won't be quite so bad, or it'll be bad in an entirely different way, and in some respects even a little worse."

For instance, the daily batches of news reports, each canceling out the last. We know and forget everything, √ even down to the percentage points. In the quavering voice we know so well, reason teaches us to look upon the latest madness as relative progress. We ought to realize that only rearmament can prepare the way for the disarmament we all long for. To inject knowledge into our democracy, they feed us to statistical charts, and we combat the energy shortage by stepping up production. We ingurgitate pills to counter pill-induced ailments. Our holidays are excuses for consumption; clearance sales mark the end of our seasons. And how clever we are: to keep food prices stable in this regionally overfed but extensively undernourished world, we pile up butter and pork mountains. That the statistical norm of fifteen million starving children a year can be exceeded in practice is demonstrated by the Cambodian mortality figures for the year that is now ending. Since we find appropriate terms for every horror, the term "nutrition gap" disposes of even multidigital death. But we have a new pope, a Polish one, who's as infallible as the Iranian Khomeini. All in all, there's no shortage of great Führer figures; a bigoted preacher in Washington and an ailing philistine in Moscow let others decide what they then proclaim to the world as their decision. Of course we still have (as trademarks of salvation) good old capitalism and good old communism; but thanks to their tried and true enmity, they are becoming (as you predicted, dear George) more and more alike: two evil old men whom we have to love, because the love they offer us refuses to be snubbed. Big Brother has a twin. The only point to be argued is whether the Big Brother twins who watch over us are uni- or diovular.

And so we grope our disconsolate way into the next century. In school essays and first novels, gloom vies with gloom. Life is written off before it has begun. Daily our poets—all masters in the quadruple *salto* of meaninglessness and other disciplines—pour out their vomit in thousands of breakfast poems. That's the way it is: since the sacred cow of enlightenment went dry, no sap can be milked from progress. Our mama's darlings want to get out as soon as the travel expenses of their peregrinations are guaranteed. Plaintively (and under protest) yesterday's revolutionaries escape into the civil service. And everyone claims, as though that were the in thing, to be afraid. Already we have group-dynamic schools that teach fear and how to overcome it. In shivering drawing rooms, we experiment with body heat. "Cuddle?" People say to each other in greeting, "Let's just quietly cuddle." Quick, develop an economical car, spread a layer of insulation over everything, give the imagination soundproof freedom of movement (in the rec room), lay in a stock of music (classical or pop), and, in expectation of things to come, think up a few attractive alternatives: If we confined ourselves to our real needs . . . If everyone took only what . . . If no one consumed more than . . . If I, provided that . . . In other words, if democratic methods won't do the . . . If democracy turns out to be inadequate . . . If you, or, let's say, I . . . If I, I and nobody else, had the say . . .

Try my hand as dictator. Pretty soon, beginning the first of the year. Usher in the eighties. That little, private hurdy-gurdy deep inside us, that primordial dream we all cherish (along with other primordial dreams) of flying, passing through walls, remaining forever a child, becoming invisible, playing God, doing it with eleven women in succession, foreseeing the future, moving mountains, or, best of all, of having the say, the uncontradicted, unrestricted say.

For only a year. That would be enough for me. After that, normal democracy could moderate my benefits. I don't want to abolish everything, just this and that. I'd deal with property as my spiritual property and that of others have been dealt with: seventy years after the author's (that's me) death, his (my) rights enter the public domain; I (as dictator) would extend this benefit by law to all earned or acquired possessions—house, factory, field —so that only the children and some of the grandchildren will be obliged to inherit it or hold it in usufruct. The ones born later will be exempt from this hereditary burden; untrammeled by Grandfather's legacy, they will be free to make a fresh start. . . .

Since I'm not a pacifist I would not, as dictator, have to abolish the Bundeswehr, but I'd convert it into a mobile army of partisans, with which any army of occupation would have to reckon in the long run. Women and children would be obligated to serve in this partisan army, as would domestic animals, Grandma and Grampa, because my partisan army, far from relying on traditional methods of warfare, will specialize in fomenting creeping, corrosive, infinitely adaptable, intimate and familiar, yieldingly soft and therefore indomitable resistance; that's how Rome was weakened and absorbed.

Naturally, if I were dictator, I'd also take popular measures, such as condemning all judges to a tenth of the prison time they mete out. I'd relieve the energy problem by means of edicts cutting all electric current at night and barring auto traffic from the cities. Furthermore (all dictators like their little jokes), I'd reintroduce the nightcaps formerly worn in Germany and unequaled for sleeping in unheated bedrooms. I wouldn't be surprised if power cuts and nightcaps proved to be just the thing to transform the decline in the German birthrate into a population explosion.

Since, having noted the failure of all attempted school reforms, I would abolish compulsory education, unmiseducated children, spurred by an uninhibited love of reading, would soon again be spelling their way through thick books. Again we'd have itinerant tutors and the attendant romances. Nationwide, for the duration of the eighties, all talk of pedagogy, all oral or written dissemination of educational concepts, old and new, and especially all mention of such words as study target, pedagogy, didactics, curriculum, educate miseducate re-educate—in short, of all words associated with the German mania for education—would be forbidden.

Once our teachers were thus emancipated, it would

remain only to abolish the prerogatives of the civil service altogether, thus conferring one more benefit on the Federal Republic of Germany—to which, as I see it, my dictatorship will be confined—and relieving the stress and strain of a fine and beautiful country. "Hereby," I would say in my edict ("Amnesty," I'd call it), "hereby I restore the freedom of these unfortunate people, who for decades have been cheated out of all risk. Never again shall they be irremediably taken care of up to the end of their lives. No longer shall they have to be ashamed of their privileges. In future no privilege shall isolate them. At last they will be permitted to taste of that delectable venture, life." Maybe I'd let myself be tempted to improve on Kaiser Wilhelm and launch the slogan of the eighties: "I no longer know civil servants, I only know Germans."

And my proposal to my Eastern neighbor-dictator would be that the two states should exchange their systems every ten years. Thus, in a spirit of compensatory justice, the Democratic Republic would have an opportunity to relax under capitalism, while the Federal Republic could drain off cholesterol under communism. The border between them would be strictly maintained, but an overarching (all-German) authority would ordain the return of property and the expropriation of the means of production. . . . This, apart from a few minor but drastic decrees, is the sum of my activity as wishful dictator. Some may say: It's not much, and there's no future in it. But for the present, I confess, I'm satisfied with these few improvements, especially since Harm Peters is waiting impatiently to have the say and to be the great dictator—"if only for one short year."

Dörte has encouraged him. On one of their latest excursions, this time to the volcano in the center of the island, she has succeeded (once again) in turning her Harm into a clown. That's the way she likes him—out of control, jumping around among the blocks of lava: the big kid. The eternal child. A Nordic picture-book hero, fighting demons and giants with a cudgel, fighting a world full of devils with his bare mouth.

Since the tourist group, after one of Wenthien's lectures—"As recently as 1963, Gunung Agung took fifteen thousand human lives"—and half an hour's walk, are taking a noonday rest over lemonade at the foot of the volcano, Harm and Dörte are left to themselves and their shenanigans. While Dörte builds a temple of lava rubble and here again dutifully deposits an offering—a bowl of rice, two, three oranges, a handful of pine nuts—Harm tests the acoustics of the natural theater under the cloud-ringed peak. "I, Harm," he cries, "have come to declare war on you spirits and demons! I will exterminate all superstitions. Come out! Show your ugly mugs! Trying to swipe my virgin! I'll show you what a German can do. Seven at one stroke. One against all. Knight, death, and devil!"

Comical as Dörte finds Harm's capers, she's not so pleased with his talk. "Harm," she cries, "please! We're guests here. You've always been a tolerant sort. You might make the volcano angry. Can't you liberate somebody or something else? You know, the oppressed and downtrodden, or the poor divided fatherland. Come on, Harm, give it a try. If you had the say in Germany. As a dictator, of course, since it's all over with democracy anyway."

Harm takes his cue. He is the stickler, the model democrat, who thinks everything is worth voting on and holds every sensible compromise sacred, he whose lips the words "grassroots democracy" cross seven times daily and for whom the ontheonehand-ontheotherhand formula has been raised to a principle, he who (with Rosa Luxemburg) is at all times prepared to stand up for the rights of those who disagree with him—accommodates himself to the role and, standing amid lava rubble, becomes a great dictator.

Naturally I keep a hand in. You won't catch me letting Harm Peters abuse his power by suppressing parties that call themselves democratic. But both Dörte and I are pleased to hear that Harm wants to abolish the church tax. "Verily I say unto you," he shouts in the direction of the cloud-swathed peak, "the Church must become poor again, as Jesus Christ was poor." But he doesn't suppress the church tax without compensation. "In its place, I ordain, an equivalent graduated tax will be levied for the benefit of the Third World countries. But not to build ungainly factories with. Certainly not! Priority will be given to agricultural development projects that will stop the flight from the land and the slummification of the cities."

Dörte is enthusiastic. "Heil Harm!" she cries. But when I try to transfer my dictatorial edict abolishing compulsory education to Dictator Harm, Schoolteacher Dörte protests violently: "That'll put us back centuries. Only the privileged classes will benefit."

And Harm, too, is rather cool to my edict, which was intended to promote creative idleness and a true love of reading, uninhibited by forced schooling. I slip him the idea of abolishing civil servants, of drawing a radical line through the German civil-service statute. Now, that would be a revolution! That would dispel the fug of the centuries! At last we'd get some air!

After some hesitation—as teachers, Harm and Dörte are, after all, civil servants—he prescribes for the West German people a radical and long-needed cure, which he formulates in my words as "the liberation of all civil servants from the burden of privileges unworthy of human beings!"

I'm surprised, though, when neither Harm nor Dörte

wants to forgo the Bundeswehr or German participation in NATO, and when both reject my project for a subversive, mobile partisan army calculated to demoralize any occupying power: "A defense based on long-term partisan activity would deter the Soviet Union more lastingly than our projected missile magic. . . ." But in the end even I am convinced by his argument against my subversive strategy: "The partisan concept goes against the grain of the German people. Rather than survive by guile underground, they would prefer to die, if need be, in open combat."

But Dictator Harm develops a staggering substitute for my crafty idea: "We keep the Bundeswehr and the NATO pact. We also carry on with disarmament through rearmament. But by the terms of an edict to take immediate effect, the entire armament of the Bundeswehr—guns, rockets, guided missiles, destroyers, all-weather pursuit planes, everything—will be replaced by meticulously copied models, thus demonstrating to our potential enemy our determination to defend ourselves and at the same time our radical rejection of war as an instrument of policy. No one will dare attack our theoretically far-superior cardboard tanks, our death-and-destruction-simulating missile mock-ups, our plastic deterrence scenery. He'd be making himself ridiculous. Nobody likes to be ridiculous, not even the Russians. And another thing: this kind of rearmament will create hundreds of thousands of new jobs."

Even after this epoch-making speech, Harm keeps going. Dörte admires him as he solves the energy problems of the eighties along my lines. Wind power and thermic pumps, giant solar screens and a rigorous energy-saving program meet with her approval. She is even willing, though with a pout, to put up with a few nuclear reactors for the transitional phase. His proposal of tapping the destructive power of all Pacific volcanoes, including the ter-

74

rible Gunung Merapi in Central Java and the local Gunung Agung, and storing it as energy, strike her as grandiose; but as soon as the great dictator Harm Peters returns to the German question and its solution, his woman freezes: What *is* he driving at? He can't be serious, And then what he says about the two German states.

For as all-German dictator, Harm Peters (after rejecting my "change of system every ten years") proclaims what he calls his medium-term program for a lasting solution of the German question.

From out of a blasted tree smothered in the lava field, he dictates: "The German people of both German states resolve of their own free will to start dying out immediately, happy in their irrevocable, social-security-sanctioned decision—yes, happy, because of the benefit they are conferring on mankind. No more children will be begotten. Every accidental pregnancy will be interrupted immediatcly. Any babies born notwithstanding will be exported without delay to Asia for adoption. In line with the German watchword "All or nothing," we take "nothing" as our target. In seventy years, to take the Biblical life span, eighty at the most, the German people will cease—with joy in their hearts—to exist. Their institutions, their system of justice and administration, their claims, and all claims against them will be declared null and void. The vacuum thus arising will be given over to nature. Forest and heath will gain space. The rivers will sigh with relief. At last the German question will have found an answer in keeping with the German character and its penchant for self-sacrifice. Naturally, the Austrians and German Swiss will be invited to participate in this medium-term program of self-effacement, but they won't have to, because my solution is German in the strictest sense. At last the fateful battle cry 'Though we be doomed to die, Germany shall live!' has found a peaceful meaning. Long live our moribund people!"

"No!" Dörte won't play. Her refusal unseats Dictator Harm. She implores the volcano to speak up: "Great and holy Gunung Agung, do you hear that!? Say something! Shut him up!"

Since the mountain keeps silent, Dörte has to do it herself. "It's nothing to joke about," she says, "now that I've finally decided to have a child." She palpates her belly, as if she were already pregnant. She says, "It's my right to have a child." She weeps among the cold lava blocks. Even Harm's half-hearted offer to postpone the big dying-out program until after the birth of their joint child fails to console her. Harm has to promise never to play dictator again. And with a grand gesture Harm promises. But the very next promise demanded of him, the promise to change his creed from No-to-baby to Yes-to-baby—"This minute, Harm, bedded on lava!"—saps his courage.

And sends him downhill. He cannot, will not. Over the rubble he runs, he leaps, and we hear him shout: "No, there are enough of us already! We have to die out! Slowly die out! It has to stop! This eternal self-perpetuation! This old-age insurance! All these medium-term prospects!"

But Dörte, who is slowly following him downhill, has got herself in hand. In this situation, she, the daughter of peasants, is strong: "Go ahead and yell. Yell your head off, kid. You'll do it in the end. You'll do it because I want you to. Because the goddess has touched me. Blessed me. Here, all over." — Whereupon she picks a bat out of her hair and pulls up her dress, disclosing a snake coiled around her left leg. Smiling, while Harm is still heard shouting downhill, she hangs the bat on a tree growing out of the lava field. The snake glides—if the camera can manage it—from leg

76

over sandaled foot, and disappears obscenely into a cleft in the rock.

This will not be cut. The bat in her hair and the snake around her leg are just as real as disarmament through rearmament or the German civil-service statute. Dörte has actually experienced all that, and because the camera is held somewhat unsteadily, Harm's super 8 film, which a while ago captured her return from the Cave of Bats, manages to convey some notion of the first bat visitation in Dörte's blond hair. Far be it from me to end the film with a Catholic manifestation of grace—in other words, to try and sell the "immaculate conception" of Dörte Peters—but as long as Harm and Dörte are on Bali, I won't go so far as to exclude other more or less miraculous phenomena.

For instance: Every evening Dörte waits on the hotel balcony for the bat to come; come it does, and nestles in her hair; whereupon Dörte writes in her diary, "The divine animal has just visited me again. Every evening annunciation. Oh, dear Harm, if you only knew how stupid your reason is. . . ."

For instance: While the tourist group is watching Balinese dances, Harm, during the famous fire dance, as the dancer dances the glowing rice straw to ashes, falls into a trance and is restrained only with difficulty from dancing barefoot in the fire. In the end Dr. Wenthien and the tax official from Wilhelmshaven escort him to the VW bus that the Sisyphus Tourist Bureau maintains on Bali for its excursions.

These are only incidental episodes thrown in as cross-cuts and needn't be explained. But a flash forward of Dörte lecturing to a meeting of portly ladies makes it clear that in Itzehoe a bat seen suddenly caught in the hair of a

Free Democratic schoolteacher is looked upon as a foreign body and not as an argument for the continuation of the Socialist-Liberal coalition.

The screaming ladies at the Café Schwarz don't calm down until Dörte explains that the bat is an incarnation of all the horrors facing them in the eighties. Whereupon she nonchalantly disentangles the flying mammal from her hair, opens a window on one side of the meeting room, and releases the bat into the late-summer evening. "That, ladies," she says, "was only my way of demonstrating that we must resolutely face up to the perils of the new decade."

This flash forward ends with applause on the part of the portly housewives and career women, for, after a dissolve or, if Schlöndorff prefers, a cut, we're back on Bali, where a bat in the hair requires no rationalization but is considered as natural as in Germany a liver sausage sealed in plastic.

There it is again, and it arouses suspicion on Bali. Harm doesn't want to forget about it. He keeps looking for his pal, good old Uwe, who was so crazy about coarse, lightly smoked liver sausage crammed into a natural casing. Harm has a hard time explaining the sausage to the Indonesian police. Besides, the suspicious object in its vacuum packaging is looking slightly under the weather. Sweating. If it weren't for Dr. Wenthien, who manages to talk Harm and his doubly endangered delicacy out of one tight place after another, the sausage would have to endure having a sample tested and be repaired with Dermicel.

Finally they're allowed to leave and take the German import with them. In the shade, to be sure, though even so the flown-in foreign body is exposed to almost ninety degrees of damp tropical heat, Dr. Wenthien explains tersely, but at some length: "On Bali, my dear fellow, the tangible is not present; but what is present remains intangible. For instance, your pal, this Herr Jensen. I know him well, yet he doesn't exist. By the way, he sends you regards. He also sends greetings to his sister, who is boarding your cat back home. He furthermore advises you to keep faith with the German school system and to take the liver sausage, for which he thanks you kindly, as a symbol of transience. But if, says your friend, you persist in delivering the Holstein delicacy in person, the addition of certain heavy crates to the luggage consignment may well involve you in some risk, thus endangering a German schoolteacher and Social Democrat who normally confines his revolutionary activity to paper. In other words, my dear Herr Peters—this is your friend's advice—let's forget about the liver sausage. Stick to tasks for which you are fitted. Don't get mixed up in the bloody battles being fought on Timor; concentrate on the German election campaign. As they say at home, on the problems of the eighties which lie before us."

This, I hope, will rid us of the liver sausage. It hasn't proved plot-fostering enough. What's left is a bundled accumulation of medium-sized conflicts and acute crises, tied with string that's beginning to come undone: a fine kettle of fish!

Dr. Wenthien expresses himself with similar concern. In connection with a fade-in of the whole tourist group— pointing at the broad, artfully terraced countryside blessed each year with three rice harvests—he says: "Undoubtedly a paradise! Get a good look at it, ladies and gentlemen, before the general expulsion begins."

And how will Sisyphus react to Orwell's decade? Should his stone be rationalized, will his stone be rationalized away?

Always when Harm Peters contemplates the emblem of the travel agency, the stone roller (taken from an ancient vase painting) on the door of the VW bus, he falls into philosophical musings and compares the labor and spiritual attitude of Sisyphus with the tasks and ethic of democratic socialism. "That's just how I see myself, Dörte. I push that stone up the mountain, and, plunk, it's down at the bottom again. Up again, down again. Over and over. All my life. I mean, we put some reform through and, hey, we think, that's not bad, but before we know it the next little reform is due. It never stops. Never, I tell you, it will never stop. The stone is always down at the bottom, waiting."

Maybe Harm in the role of Sisyphus could be drawn into our picture, demonstrating his existential reformism with a medium-sized boulder on the mountainous lava field that just witnessed him as dictator. ("Look, Dörte," groans the struggling Harm, "this is my seventh try at pension reform.")

Or we see him pushing an enormous boulder up the side of the Brokdorf dike (the disposal of nuclear waste!), see how the stone, no sooner has Harm pushed it to the top, gets restless (in slow motion) of its own accord and starts rolling downhill; we see Harm pushing and pushing, while Dörte shouts: "Go on, Harm! Don't give up! You'll make it. Keep at it. That's the only way we'll beat the eighties. Accept the challenge. No freaking out. Go on! Don't weaken! Forward! Yes to the stone. Look at this. Even our travel brochure says so: 'Sisyphus is master of his fate. That is his secret joy. His stone is his fate!'"

And Harm listens to Dörte and to Camus. Orwell can't scare him. Harm is the absurd hero battling the absurd; he is the hero of history.

Albert Camus published his essay in 1942, in the middle of the war. I read *The Myth of Sisyphus* in the early fifties. But even before that, with no knowledge of the so-called absurd, stupid as the war left me, I was on intimate terms with all the questions of being, hence with existentialism. And later, when the concept of the absurd became personified for me, when (fed up with the Christian-Marxist muck about hope) I saw the cheery stone roller as a man who encouraged us to roll stones in vain, to scoff at punishment and damnation—so then I found myself a stone and was happy with it. It gives me purpose. It is what it is. No God, no gods can take it away from me; unless they capitulate to Sisyphus and leave the stone on the mountaintop. That would be boring and not worth wishing for.

But what is my stone? The toil of piling words on √ words? The book that follows book that follows book? Or the German uphill task of securing a bit of freedom for stone rollers (and suchlike absurd fools). Or love, with all its epileptic fits? Or the fight for justice, that boulder so hard to push upward and so ready to tumble?

All this makes my stone round and jagged. I see it tipping, in thoughts I anticipate its fall. It never disappoints me. It doesn't want to be freed from me nor I from it. It is human, in my measure. It is also my God, who without me does not exist. No heavenly Jerusalem can take its place, no earthly paradise make it useless. Therefore I scoff at any promise that my stone will reach the top and rest there once and for all. But I also laugh at the stone, which wants to make me the hero of its overand-overagain. "Look, stone," I say. "See how lightly I take you. You are so absurd and so used to me that you've become my trademark. Sisyphus is a good advertisement. You are a good traveling companion."

6

The First World War, so they say, was kindled in the Bosnian city of Sarajevo, and the Second sparked off in my home town of Danzig: now Tehran seems to fill the bill. Whenever people stop talking about family rubbish or babbling about the price of gold and its ups and downs, they go on interminably about the interminable hostage business—that localized crisis. It can't be denied, humans have progressed: they can count to three.

Ought I now, because the might of the Americans and Russians has taught us to tremble and (since Vietnam and Prague) has been dictating its brand of morality, to give up my puns, let all remaining merriment go sour, give the Muses notice, and snuff out the spark of life in my— admittedly goofy—headbirths before they've even learned to croak "Papa" and "Mama"? That would be showing respect for stupid might. Acknowledging its rotten morality. Accepting a logic that has made Bosnian Sarajevo notorious and destroyed my home town of Danzig, whereas I, with words alone, have resuscitated the city of Danzig, which is now called Gdańsk. None of the mighty can hold a candle to me. They're ridiculous and they're bunglers to boot. Haughtily I deny them the right to bother me when I'm writing. .

Because, you see, I want everything to take place at once (on paper as in my head). The journey to Asia is drawing to an end, but I still see Dörte at home, studying the Sisyphus prospectus. "Hey, look at this! They even quote Camus's *Myth of Sisyphus* in their advertising."

While Dörte quotes the literary come-on—"The struggle against mountaintops can fill a human heart . . ."—I hear Dr. Wenthien on Bali, this time in the precinct of a Hindu temple, continuing the quotation: "We must think of Sisyphus as a happy man."

And though shortly before starting out Harm says, "Sure thing. We'll have the baby. Stop talking ourselves into the loony bin. I'm a hundred percent in favor. We'll do it on Bali"—I hear him vacillate at the Kuta Beach Hotel: "Yes, yes! I said it. Sure. But things aren't the same any more. Anyway, there's no hurry. Got to come to terms with all this. You know, this place and all. It's been quite a shock, you know."

Dörte feels that she's really been had. Troubled, she wraps her Hindu fertility doodad in layers of batik—"I'm sorry, I shouldn't carry on so, I admit it's silly"—very much as, in the excitement of her departure from Itzehoe, she packed her freshly ironed odds and ends: "And if I come home pregnant, I'll fling myself right into the electoral campaign. Maternity benefits for working women and so on . . ."

Harm, on the other hand, had set out with the intention of leaving the "strain of West German politics" at home. But whether he's walking on the beach or buying the last souvenirs, such as "a snake bracelet for dear Dörte," politics always butts in: "I've learned a lot on this trip.

Beginning in Bombay. When we get back, I'll reduce it to basic principles. Notes on the North-South differential. It's got to be made perfectly clear. As part of our election campaign."

Overcrowded as Dörte's and Harm's heads are with other monsters, the antedated happening they have dragged along with them, the election campaign traveling in Harm's pocket calendar, should go right on (if the world situation doesn't prevent us from shooting our film during the summer travel season). Under beach palms, he plans his activities: "September 2, morning drinks in Kellinghusen. September 5, symposium with ecologists in Wilster. September 12, young voters' meeting in Glückstadt. September 17, street meeting in the pedestrian zone . . ."

On the beach facing the surf, or confronting a paddling of ducks paddling about in a rice paddy, wherever he finds an opposite number, I have Harm practice electioneering. Most recently on Bali—while Dörte is off on her religious maternity excursions—I hear him inveighing against Strauss or, ignoring Strauss, against Stoltenberg and Albrecht: "What have these gentlemen to offer us for the eighties!"

Strong statements are followed by complicated ontheonehand-ontheotherhand dissertations on the comprehensive school and the future of the North German Radio, on defense of the environment and the problems of nuclear-waste disposal. From a safe distance, he grinds out a number of his standard formulations: "Our carefully considered yes to the limited development of nuclear energy goes hand in hand with an unequivocal no to reprocessing plants."

Or: "The necessity of rearming NATO must not cause us to lose sight of our central purpose, disarmament." And time and time again he demands that "the industrial nations shoulder their responsibility for the Third World."

While off to one side old women drag splintered shells out of the surf as they do day in, day out, he hopes for change: "The rich get richer and the poor get poorer. We must see to it that those words, so true of the seventies, do not apply to the eighties."

And suchlike maxims. I'm sure Volker Schlöndorff will find a way of having the sentences hurled at the tepid surf or the paddling of ducks dissolve into forward-flashed applause or boos over morning drinks in Kellinghusen, during the young voters' meeting, in a smoke-filled bar in Wilster. As in the quarrel over the headbirth baby, time is suspended, place telescopes with place, everything is made present; only the liver sausage—there it is again—is capable of development, of change: it's getting moldy. Everything else can be dragged from Itzehoe to Asia and back. Everything else fits here as well as there. What here needs to be drained, there demands to be irrigated: the heavy soil of the Wilstermarsch, the paddy fields of the tourist island. And mightn't the swampy slum of Klong Toei be transplanted from Bangkok to the fenced-in area of the projected nuclear power plant in Brokdorf?

At least they're equally flat. And besides, such a move has a future. So, ignoring the logistical problem, we'll show (after a cut or a dissolve) fifty thousand Southeast Asian slum dwellers penned into the construction site behind the Elbe dike. Board and corrugated-iron shacks propped up on stilts along ramshackle footbridges traversing mud, dung, and sewage, while roundabout cows and calves graze on rich pastures. Saturated green, as though squeezed from the tube. Overhead, the North German sky.

Harm and Dörte see all this from the dike, or else, while watching each other from the dike, re-enact their

86

Sisyphus-promoted night in the slum. ("Experience the real unvarnished Asia!") All this is imaginable and therefore real. ("From a purely intellectual standpoint," says Harm.) Consequently, they find no difficulty in transposing themselves at any time from Bombay or their dream island into their classrooms at the Kaiser Karl School (KKS for short). And instantly they find themselves exposed to the pupils' questions: "How was the trip?" — "Are you finally pregnant?" — "When is your wife getting her baby?" — "What? False alarm?" — "Are we Germans to die out, while the Indians and Chinese just go on multiplying?"

To these (as Harm and Dörte complain to their tour guide) aggressive schoolchildren's questions, most of which bubble up lazily as though from an interrupted doze, Dr. Wenthien could be ready with an answer to be dispensed while walking and therefore long enough to widen the garden of the Kuta Beach Hotel: "That, children, is only a beginning. Worse is yet to come. The travel-mad Indians, the Egyptian fellahin, the plethoric Mexicans and Javanese, let's say seven percent of a billion Chinese, will do up their bundles, gird up their loins, leave their all-too-sunny homelands, and, still plentiful despite predictable losses en route, trickle into our country; at first gradually, in batches, then in waves, and finally in an unstemmable flood. You know arithmetic, children, you've learned from Herr and Frau Peters that by the year 2000 the world population will have swollen to just seven billion, four billion of whom will be packed into Asia. Each day there are a hundred seventy thousand more of us humans. They've got to go somewhere. These surpluses have an unerring sense of direction. Europe, with its social system, its calligraphed human rights, and its Christian guilty conscience, offers itself. Don't worry, children. These people are humble and industrious. They will lighten our work load. They learn more quickly than we do. And they don't take up much space. They can fit a large family into two rooms. They don't need rec rooms. They will multiply in the normal way, no headbirths for them. They will produce a generation we can build on. While you, dear children, will be able to rest, relax, and misbehave. It has begun already, in England, France, and here. They get used to the climate in no time. Why shouldn't kids from Java get to feel like Germans? Why shouldn't we, intelligent as we would like to be, learn a little colloquial Chinese, why should we content ourselves with our usual basic German? Who would want to prevent our sparse progeny—you, my dear children, and later on your only-children—from intermarrying with the progeny of Upper Egyptian fellahin and Mexican mestizos? The slender vivacity of the coastal Chinese women, the gentleness of Sundanese men will be desired, the mystical spice of India will be sought after. Don't worry, children, the Germans won't die out. In a version refined by crossbreeding they will be prolific, pretty soon there'll be two, three hundred million of us. The world will—how shall I put it—absorb the Germans. To be German will be to partake of the world. Once again we'll amount to something. — What? What's this I hear? You don't want to crossbreed? You Germanic-Slavic-Celtic hybrids want to keep your racial purity? You subsidized imbeciles want to limit yourselves, to survive in your present limited state? We want to stay the way we are, you yell. Insulated. Shut up shop! Seal ourselves off! Wall ourselves in! Don't make me laugh. As if walls were any use in this day and age! As if walls could stem the brown-yellow-black flood. We've already got a wall running straight through. Expertly built, lethally solid. Has this wall helped the few Germans over there and the steadily fewer Germans over here to help or oppose one another? Has this wall ever been good for anything but having more and more holes bored into it—on both sides? The wall must go! you shouted. Exactly, children. Walls are obsolete.

We saw that on our trip. On the section of the Chinese Wall near Peking that has been opened to domestic and foreign tourists, I took several pictures of Ute: she on the lower edge of the picture with her Baltic unquiet hair, while behind her the wall, rigid, immovable (and yet from the very start futile), crawls in bolder and bolder foreshortenings over mountain ridges. Has it, have other barriers prevented the Chinese worldwide from gathering on the Feast of the Moon to eat the moon cake, whose sweetness was equally sweet to us in Canton, Hong Kong, and Singapore? And couldn't Dr. Wenthien, while predicting his ethnic migrations, weave in this detail: "Soon, dear children, that too-sweet Chinese moon cake will be available all over Germany, but that shouldn't spoil our taste for crumb cake."

Or the walls in the waterfront section of Manila, population one and a half million. They were built in the late sixties, when Pope Paul visited the Catholic Philippines and their Catholic dictator, Marcos, who had the main street, which bounds far-flung slum areas, walled off, for fear that the sight of such unholy misery would offend the Holy Father's eyes. (These prodigious walls were also useless; for if the misery to the left and right had not been concealed from the Holy Father, he wouldn't have known what to make of it, or he would have interpreted it as God's will and included it in his prayers. Popes are past masters at that sort of welfare work.)

Walls can be compared. They differ only superficially.

The medieval ones, including the Chinese, were built for eternity, regardless of the cost; the blind that screened the papal eyes from the slums of Manila, the masonry in which realistic socialism is immured in Berlin, and the slabs of concrete joined to form a wall around the construction site for the Brokdorf nuclear power plant in the Wilstermarsch were built for the present, hence in haste. From this Dr. Wenthien should draw further pedagogical inferences in his conversation with Harm and Dörte Peters. For the pupils of the Kaiser Karl School in Itzehoe are still concerned about their future. They don't want to become foreign-dominated hybridized Orwellian Eurasians. (They stamp their feet and pound their desks with their fists. "It gives us the creeps!" shouts one of the boys.)

"Very well, dear children," Wenthien might say in the shade of the palm trees, "you're dead set on walling yourselves in. I understand. I think it's worth considering myself. And I'm sure there are Western and Eastern and possibly joint East-Western contingency staffs toying with plans for walling off the industrial nations. Because if we want to protect our still-quarrelsome East-West structure— in other words, the North—against a reverse *Völkerwanderung* pouring in from the South, it would be necessary to devise a new wall technology—though its failure is virtually predictable. After all, we have more knowledge than we are at present able to apply. Our satellite surveillance. Our early-warning systems. Our nuclear by-products. What our great minds have thought up. All that, children, gives grounds for hope. One might, for example, conceive of several deeply echeloned radiation walls, starting at the Sino-Russian border, taking in the Arabo-Iranian oil region, skirting the Mediterranean coast of Africa, describing a wide arc around the Iberian peninsula, and

the wall gap

protecting all Europe, or else screening off the North Atlantic and linking up with a similarly programmed American radiation wall. It would be that simple. Of course, we could draw Japan and South Korea into our protected cultural sphere. And, naturally, there would be sluice gates in our radiation wall, passages for free trade, but also for occasional southbound punitive expeditions—in case, for instance, someone tries to interfere with our peaceful exploitation of raw materials outside our national boundaries. The protection of our air space is already highly developed; to screen it off completely would be child's play, provided the East-West conflict kept leveling off. And why shouldn't it? Even if capitalism and communism step on each other's toes, my dear children, they're the same pair of shoes. Working together, they'll be capable of greater effort. Because total radiation screening doesn't mean isolationism. Far from it. We shall remain open to the world. Our development programs, our world famine relief, our unstinting charities, our Christian-Marxist social utopias will still be on offer. Who would dare to hold back! Our economic system wouldn't think of depriving the world of its multinational benefits. Certainly not! We're not self-sufficient. For though on the one hand we screen ourselves off, on the other hand we travel. I don't want you growing up to be stay-at-homes; I want you to be cosmopolitans. Just so we don't let ourselves be submerged by foreign influences. Our home-grown minority problems are already troublesome enough. We Germans want to go on being surveyable, countable, not some numberless mass. After all, we're not Indians, fellahin, Chinese, or mestizos. We've already got Turks enough! We don't intermarry. We wall ourselves off. We preserve our limitations. Undismayed, we die out. And what used to be called the Iron Curtain—never mind, children, we understand each other. Only the azimuth has changed. Ridiculous, all these bugaboos. Just let the eighties come!"

"Orwell willing!" Harm Peters, who may after all have read this author, could add to Wenthien's last sentence. When Wenthien's words seek out their audience on the hotel terrace that evening (over a glass of freshly squeezed orange juice), the whole tourist group should be assembled. Cries such as "Dreadful!" or "He's damn right!" could be distributed. The pastor's widow could say, "Lucky me! I won't live to see it!" The tax official from Wilhelmshaven could say, "A cheerful prospect!" and one of the mid-fortyish men: "Hear, hear!"

Dr. Wenthien knows his Asia. He cites figures showing that Java is aptly called an "overloaded ship." Dutch colonial history can be coaxed out of him, dates and all, down to the last pillaging expedition. "In December 1906, the Balinese rajahs and members of their families and households were driven to suicide by the hundreds. Responsible for this act of purification was Royal Dutch General Van de Velde. . . ." And he also knows all about the present corruption, the business deals of the President's family—Mrs. Suharto in the forefront—down to their West German entanglements: "The Gutehoffnung Metal Works of Hanover holds quite a few shares."

As a sideline, Wenthien is father confessor to our group. The mid-fortyish couples, the tax official, the statuesque mother and sickly daughter come to him with their aches, pains, and climatic difficulties; their existential complaints and spells of nausea end in his lap. Harm and Dörte Peters come to him, the great guru and world-crisis specialist who (presumably) is mixed up in the international arms traffic, with their headbirths. Now, toward the end of their trip, with increasing urgency.

And yet, within partnerly limits, they truly care for

each other. She rinses the sand not only out of her bikini, but out of his swimming trunks as well. He pampers her every morning by bringing her a coconut with a straw in it. Even if they can't talk to each other any more, they still discuss controversial matters. And according to Dörte's diary, to which she confides everything, including her desire for more things than a child, their relationship is not in crisis. Both of them think and say, "We're made for each other." But because Harm has been holding back in bed since Dörte's "religious freak-out"—"I can't do it, I tell you! I'm not a stud bull!"—Dörte unburdens herself to Dr. Wenthien.

She says: "I'd like to have a frank talk with you. In my situation I can forget about modesty. Right now would be the best time, ovulationwise. I mean, if we want it to take —and this time, really, it has to take—but then I don't know how, but today or tomorrow I'd have to . . ."

Dr. Wenthien smiles. He understands. Nothing human is alien to him. He says: "I, too, will speak frankly. Paternity is an arbitrary concept. On Sumatra there are regions, and the same is true of Dravidian India, where the father—well, let's say the father plays a very marginal role. Does it absolutely have to be your very charming husband, your pigheaded Harm?"

Before Dörte Peters can misinterpret this "objective analysis" as an altruistic offer and reject it, the tour guide explains at greater length. "Look around you, my dear Frau Peters. These gentle Balinese youths. The grace of their movements. Their playful, undemanding nature—all they want from anyone is a little money for gas. An excellent race, by the way, these Malayan Sundanese. I see you've been reading Vicki Baum's *Love and Death on Bali*, apparently with enthusiasm. A subtle masterpiece. The way Lambon the dancer, though the rajah's favorite wife, keeps going back to her Raka, the great dancer . . ."

Here Wenthien, after leafing through the borrowed paperback, possibly quoting one or two passages and returning it to Dörte, might point with a sweeping gesture at a group of youths outside the hotel, waiting with their Kawasakis for customers. "Just go to it, my dear Frau Peters. As the night quickly falls, a little stroll down the farflung beach. And then beneath the Southern Cross . . ."

But this I don't want: this rapid trip routine. I don't want Dörte Peters latching on to one of those tender-limbed youths and whishing across the quickly darkening, soon deserted beach, heading for dunes, starry tent, ovulation, and spermatic happiness. I don't want any surprises springing from triangle situations. The Yes-to-baby No-to-baby question, this game of will-we-won't-we, must be decided by Harm and Dörte alone. No wind-blown seed will fertilize this field. And besides, Dörte is incapable of taking a film-worthy plunge.

True, she takes a few steps toward the waiting youths, possibly she goes right up to them with Nordic determination, picks out one, the right one, of the gentle-eyed youths, maybe she even makes up her mind (how charmingly he smiles) and gives her wish full steam—to wit: she goes on, points beach- and duneward, whisks away with the youth, and demonstrates her identity with flying hair—but after a protracted closeup and a long shot of the beach, and before the pair vanish in the evening mist, the film starts running backward: rear wheel in the lead, her hair blowing forward, the purring Kawasaki carries her back, crablike, to the group of youths outside the hotel. Dörte gets off as she got on. The charming smile is repeatable. She gives the gentle-eyed youth a farewell glance, rolls up her wish, walks backward with Nordic determination, and ends up standing beside Dr. Wenthien again.

94

With her paperback in hand, Dörte Peters, after pushing her wish phantasms to the edge of her principles, says negligently to the tour guide: "Ah, yes, the beautiful Lambon's devotion to Raka the dancer. The play of their bodies. Two dragonflies. It would be beautiful. And it's not any sort of moral scruples. It's just my principles. Stupid, I know. But what can I do? Do you understand?"

Dr. Wenthien understands everything. "Too bad about your ovulation," he says. And: "Tomorrow we'll have to start thinking about packing. Do make sure your luggage isn't overweight."

Ours was overweight in Cairo, but the Lufthansa people were indulgent (seeing that the plane was two hours late), so there was no extra charge. We hung around the waiting room with the Schlöndorffs, who had shown their film in Djakarta, Tel Aviv, and lastly in Cairo, and whose trip was also drawing to a close. Another coffee. Volker combed the souvenir shops for a pharaoh's ring but couldn't find anything he liked. As usual in such situations, Ute knitted, needle after needle, on a muffler for me in graduated earth colors. Margarethe thought she'd bring some knitting on her next trip. ("How long will it be? Since when has it been growing?")

Ute had started the muffler on the train from Shanghai to Kweilin, while a young Chinese teacher of German was telling us about the Cultural Revolution and its consequences. Terraced rice paddies repeated themselves on both sides of the train. Wet tillage. The broad, system-outliving straw hats of the industriously crouching farm workers. Pure profit. All made by human hands. While simultaneously Ute's intercontinental knitting needles . . .

When, after a stop in Canton, where the Feast of the Moon was being celebrated, we took the train out of the People's Republic of China and into the Western showpiece of Hong Kong, the shawl grew a foot, though at the head end of every car in the heavily air-conditioned tourist train capitalist television was being run to get the travelers used to it, and even the Red Chinese conductresses had an eye for the commercials. Ute kept right at it. Unswervingly she stuck to the thread. On the flight to Singapore, in the waiting room of the Singapore airport, then during the flight to Manila, whenever space was overcome by time, my muffler grew visibly under her hands. And when we flew to Cairo, surrounded for seventeen hours by Philippine Moslems on their way to Mecca, it took on an imposing but not yet definitive length.

I remembered other trips and told the Schlöndorffs about the time the previous year when Ute's ball of wool fell off her lap and rolled down the center aisle in the direction of the cockpit as, shortly before the fueling stop in Anchorage, the plane tilted gently Alaska-ward. An anachronistic thing to happen. Instantly alerted, a hostess rolled the ball up again (toward us). Ute thanked her. Literary parallels occurred to me. The hostess expressed the opinion that what with all the time they spent waiting, air hostesses should be supplied with wool and their training should include a course in knitting.

So I think I'll suggest to Volker that we have Dörte Peters, or the tall, Baltic-blond actress who takes her part, knit or crochet during the trip to Asia, maybe baby things, which Harm Peters calls silly or at least premature: "Why not wait? You're making me superstitious. Or knit something for me. A long muffler in graduated earth colors: ocher, brown, umber."

And no matter what she's knitting or crocheting, the ball of knitting wool or crocheting yarn could fall off her lap. On one of their flights, preferably on the homeward flight, shortly before the fueling stop in Karachi, the ball

96

rolls down the aisle in the direction of the cockpit. And the eye of the hostess—in other words, the camera—catches the rolling ball, which in spite of the yarn it's losing gets bigger and bigger. Dörte likewise thanks the hostess.

For, knowledgeably as she discusses the problems of education, local politics, and energy, undeviatingly as she looks upon herself as a career woman, there's no reason why Dörte Peters shouldn't knit or crochet. She justifies her feminine bent; several times at women's meetings she has clarified her "position," rejecting the "bigotry of wrongheaded liberation": "I'm a woman. And, being a woman, I like to knit. Wouldn't it be silly if in the name of equal rights I were to insist on my husband's taking up knitting or crocheting. The fact is, he has the male mania for collecting, which I have not. But I say to myself, let him collect all he likes if it makes him happy. . . ."

So their luggage could be overweight. Harm has not only picked up lightweight sea shells and snail shells on the beaches, but also gathered strange roots and grotesquely shaped lava rocks from the lava fields, and he is determined to drag all his treasures home to Itzehoe.

"Too much and too heavy," says Dörte. He is obliged to discard the larger pieces. His remark—"Oh, well, you're having to do without what you most wanted to take home" —strikes Dörte as "horribly insulting" and she reacts by slapping his face. His face slapped, Harm Peters apologizes: "I'm sorry. Honestly." Both cry a little.

Then they go on with their packing. All the rubbish they're taking home with them. The batik for Monika. Thai silk for Harm's mother. Dörte's father is expected to be delighted with a Malay kris. And another bit of cloth. And a salad fork and spoon for Dörte's mother. And suddenly the liver sausage crops up again.

It's lying in the refrigerator. Its condition is dubious.

We haven't got rid of it. Because Harm's old pal Uwe Jensen couldn't be found. Because I rejected arms smuggling as a plot element. Because the Indonesian police returned the suspicious sausage after the sample had been tested. Because the wound in the casing was healed with Dermicel. Because Harm rejects Dörte's suggestion of burying the sausage in the sand. Because I've run out of ideas on the subject. So it stays in the refrigerator. Or they take it with them, fly it back to the German Federal Republic. Like the Yes-to-baby No-to-baby question they've also brought with them. Another unsolved problem.

When the nonstop flight from Cairo to Munich was finally announced, Volker Schlöndorff and I saw something we didn't wholly believe until we exchanged notes during the flight: on the way to the passport inspection desk there stands an above-lifesize Henry Mooresque statue of a mother goddess, designed to imprint a symbol of fertility, of the fruitful womb, upon the minds of all those departing from the overpopulated land of Egypt. Yes, we know the figures.

7

How we listen to and challenge each other. How I take no notes and he fills pad after pad. Two craftsmen hiding behind their tools. (When he was shooting *The Tin Drum*, I was entered in his diary as a nuisance factor; now I make use of his resistance.)

"Can't you make me more fictitious?" — Sure, but how? Though always on his way somewhere, he's always present. The invited guest brings cold-pressed olive oil. Should I call him "master," as though I had invented him? The master with the note pads visits the master without a note pad and brings cold-pressed olive oil. — Welcome! I've long been hoping for someone who doesn't carry on like a genius. We don't have to compete. We amuse ourselves with details. Our temperaments are gratifyingly different.

"Harm and Dörte," says Volker Schlöndorff, "ought to leave something with friends back in Itzehoe. Why not a cat?" "I," I say, "will consider the cat in the third draft of my manuscript: how they make arrangements for their cat before leaving and find it on their return. . . ."

99

. . . but right now, before they take off, I give some thought to my thing about teachers. What did they do to me? What bad marks am I still afraid of? What gripes me about German pedagogues? Why do their curriculums and early-imprint systems rub me the wrong way?

It was a mistake to imagine that *Cat and Mouse* would abreact my schoolboy sorrows. I never run out of teachers. I can't let them be: Fräulein Spollenhauer tries to educate Oskar; in *Dog Years*, Brunies sucks his cough drops; in *Local Anaesthetic*, Teacher Starusch suffers from headaches; in *The Diary of a Snail*, Hermann Ott remains a teacher even when holed up in a cellar; even the Flounder turns out to be a pedagogue; and now these two teachers from Holstein . . .

Maybe what prevents me from letting them be is that my growing children bring school into the house day after day: the generation-spanning fed-upness, the to-do over grades, the search, straying now to the right and now to the left, for meaning, the fug that stinks up every cheerful breath of air! — And yet Dörte and Harm took up teaching with the best of intentions. . . .

They are no longer wholly in the island paradise. Their last day of room and board, M.A.P. That night the plane is to carry them home from Bali (with fuel stops). Their packed bags are waiting in the hotel lobby, ready to go. Dörte is sitting in the half-shade of the palm trees, reading. Harm is sticking to the statuesque mother's sickly daughter in the garden bar of the Kuta Beach Hotel. Since garden paths have to be raked, the paths leading to the beach and to the bar are being raked. Dr. Wenthien is going about among the members of the Sisyphus tourist group, distributing advice. The lined-up suitcases have been fitted with tags. As usual, the gentle-eyed youths are waiting with their Kawasakis for customers. Off to one side, Balinese women are carrying little bowls of rice to offer up at the shrine. Dörte is reading the novel she has borrowed. Under the holy tree, offerings are offered. Harm drinks his third Campari with the sickly daughter. The mid-fortyish couples are writing their last postcards. Dr. Wenthien advises them all against overtipping. A cage in the middle of the hotel garden is inhabited. The Balinese women look past and through the tourists. One of the trees on the sand dune is holy. Looking up from her borrowed book, Dörte sees the native women with their offerings. An old man is raking the paths. Wenthien back and forth in wrinkled trousers. Two monkeys are rattling the bars of their cage. Dörte speeds up her reading. Harm tries to make a pass at the sickly daughter. More and more women with bowls of rice. Dr. Wenthien says, "There's still plenty of time." Elsewhere he says, "The bus leaves at five-thirty." Dörte drinks out of a young coconut through a straw. The rattling monkeys, who are now delousing each other. The sickly daughter has to go back to her room—to get something. The rake and its sound. Harm does not remain seated with his Campari. The mid-fortyish couples have a system—one writes postcards, the other stamps them. The light under the palm trees. Wenthien's advice. The open page of the paperback shows two hands holding a half coconut shell. The near-empty Campari glasses are removed from the bar. The monkeys. The overdecorated shrine. The harmonizing couples. Now the sound of the rake is missing. Now Wenthien is explaining the world situation to the tax official from Wilhelmshaven. Dörte reading. Last stamps. "The Russians," says Wenthien. A sudden breeze in the palms. The tagged suitcases are taken away. Dörte shuts her book. Wenthien claps his hands. So do the monkeys in the cage. Overtipping is avoided. The tourist group assembles. Harm and the sickly daughter have insouciantly rejoined the group. Coconut shell and straw are left behind. Dörte walks long-legged over raked paths. Dr. Wenthien promises to mail the postcards at the airport. Someone (the camera begins by showing running brown legs), a houseboy, runs after someone (Harm) with a forgotten something (the vacuum-packed liver sausage). Before getting into the Sisyphus bus, Dörte waves at the gentle-eyed youths on their Kawasakis. There's room in Harm's hand luggage for the liver sausage. In the bus, or possibly at the airport, Dörte tries to return Dr. Wenthien's paperback, though she "hasn't quite finished it." But the tour guide makes her a present of it. "A little memento, dear Frau Peters. Because, you see, we both love Bali, this paradise that will soon be lost forever. . . ."

I suppose I should (I don't want to) detail every scene along these lines. Room should be left for accidents. No indication of where the pastor's widow makes inappropriate remarks at the right moment. Nothing about the slight coolness between the late-thirtyish girl friends. Nor do I know whether Dörte, as soon as she is safety-belted, goes on reading. But before our teacher couple flies off, leaving Dr. Wenthien behind with another Sisyphus group which has just arrived, I should like to throw in certain misgivings, deductions, and conjectures; once the Singapore Airlines plane takes off, it will be too late for digressions.

What am I letting myself in for? The present. In the fifties and early sixties, when I wrote extensively about the past, the critics shouted: Bravo! The past must be overcome. From a distance, that is! Once upon a time.

In the late sixties and early seventies, when I wrote about the present—the 1969 election campaign, for instance—the critics shouted: Phooey! This undistanced involvement with the present! This blatant political position! That's not how we want him. That's not what we expect of him.

In the late seventies, when (again extensively) I amalgamated the Stone Age and ensuing periods with the present, the critics cried out: At last! He has re-emerged. Clearly he has given up, he is escaping into the past. This is how we like him. He owed it to himself and us.

If now, shortly before the inception of the eighties, I am once again biting (undistanced) into the present—though Strauss is a relic of the fifties—the critics will shout (guess what?): Here it comes! His contribution to the election campaign. He just can't stop. And what does he mean by "headbirths"? Hasn't he fathered plenty of children? What right has he to talk? How can he understand childlessness as a social trend? That's a subject for young writers. He should stick to his past, his once-upon-a-time.

All that is true. We've learned in school that the present comes after the past and is followed by the future. But I work with a fourth tense, the paspresenture. That's why my form gets untidy. On my paper more is possible. Here only chaos foments order. Here even holes are contents. And loose threads are threads that have been left radically untied. Here everything doesn't have to come out even. That's why the Wenthien phenomenon has not been clarified. The liver sausage lives on as luggage without revealing its deeper meaning. But if I neglect the features of Harm and Dörte Peters, outfitting him with no squint and her with no gap between her front teeth, it's for a reason. Schlöndorff will fill in these clearly circumscribed blanks with the facial expressions of two actors, but this much is definite: he should be ash blond and she Baltic blond.

And it would be good if both actors were not authentically mumbling amateurs, but trained in diction and masters of the Holstein accent. And both actors should bring a capacity for comedy to their solemn labors, for the occasional despair of my educators makes me laugh. And I would like Dr. Wenthien, who has now been left behind at the Denpasar airport, not to be demonic or at all times subtly opaque, but to be as naïvely shrewd and as crudely wise as devils and demons in the role of tour guide are bound to be.

What still remains for me to add: the regularity, built into the Yes-to-baby No-to-baby dilemma, with which the adoption of a child is considered and rejected. As in Itzehoe, so in Bombay, Bangkok, and Bali: wherever Harm and Dörte, out of fear of the future or in expectation of slightly improved prospects, succumbing to convenience or to a longing for parental responsibility, want or do not want a child, this supplementary question arises. For every time they decide unanimously not to bring a child into this already overpopulated world by the use of their own loins and womb, a vestige of discontent is left at the bottom of the cup: "We could, though. I mean, by socially committing ourselves. And considering our financial circumstances . . ."

But their altruism has limits. In the midst of begging Indian children, who touch the hem of her skirt and grab at his hands, he says: "Help yourself. There are plenty to choose from, and getting to be more and more. But please, I ask you, only one of the five hundred, five hundred thousand, five million . . ."

And when, surprised by a tropical shower, they find themselves beneath a corrugated-iron roof with some Indonesian children, Dörte says: "Which should it be? This one or that one? But that's selection. The Buchenwald ramp, with a humanitarian touch. To choose one child is to abandon all the rest, to let them perish." And while they escape into a covered bicycle ricksha, Harm names every possible consequence of an adoption: "The child will always be a foreigner. The usual teasing. And beatings. Think of the Turkish schoolchildren in Itzehoe. . . ."

Whereupon, as usual when they have answered the adoption question in the negative, they consider the possibility of moving Harm's mother from Hademarschen to their roomy prewar apartment, only to reject this act of social responsibility as well. "Take my word for it," says Dörte. "Mother would never get used to living with us." "Maybe she would," says Harm, "if we had a child."

Again no decision. Only the daily headbirth. "Then, under acceptable conditions," he says in the ricksha, "it would be better to have a child of our own." "Or," says she, "we'll take your mother after all."

And when Harm Peters bids Dr. Wenthien good-bye at the airport, he says something like this: "Well, maybe we'll pull it off next trip. Through Central Africa or something. In that case, great master, we'll send you a postcard."

They fly. They fly as we flew. We got back in the fall of 1979; Harm and Dörte's flight is postdated to late August 1980. The four of us, they and we, drag our Asian doodads to Europe. We hadn't managed (they on Bali, we in China) to get rid of our German leftovers. No sooner landed, my teacher couple are sucked into the election campaign: the dates have already been set. To us the West German everyday was immediately served up: the narrowness, the blatant consumption, the deep-rooted antagonisms, the warmed-over fears, the cautious conditionals of pundits intent on safeguarding themselves on all sides: "I should think . . . I should think . . ."

Because Harm and Dörte Peters are my headbirths, I put things into their cradle that concern me—for instance, the continuation of the Brokdorf trial on Monday, November 26, 1979, in Schleswig. Since they fly home from Bali to Itzehoe nine months after the end of the trial, they must know the (to me unknown) outcome: whether or not the nuclear power plant in Brokdorf is being built, and when the court's decision went into effect.

A wet, cold day. She had excused herself from school. I was expecting her and she came. The peasant's educated daughter. Later, in the midday break, we talked. Possibilities crackled between us. But that would only have taken our minds off the big thing: the trial.

On the first day I, with my brown press card, had no trouble getting in, but Dörte had difficulty in procuring a yellow admission card. Together we witnessed the helplessness of the presiding judge, Feist, who first, with the help of the police, cleared the visitors' section of the courtroom (because of overcrowding and disorder), then allowed the hall to fill up again after several specially trained policemen had photographed the public individually and in groups in the entrance and on the stairs for identification purposes. This, in Newspeak, is called "gathering intelligence." That's how Dörte and I got into the card file. (In the picture we're smiling at each other like old friends.)

Dörte Peters agreed with me that the mayor of Wewelsfleth championed the cause of the plaintiffs (four townships and two hundred fifty individual complainants) more passionately and knowledgeably than did their lawyers. But while I listened without comment, she shouted several times, "Right!"

When Dörte clapped after Mayor Sachse's speech and shouted, "We won't let them wreck Wilstermarsch!" she and other foes of nuclear energy were warned by the presiding judge: "We have means of conducting this trial in a manner both dignified and productive."

Whereupon we listened (I in silence, Dörte barely muttering under her breath) to the intricate pronouncements of the entrepreneurial party—six or seven lawyers representing the *Land* of Schleswig-Holstein and the construction firms. We heard them question the right of the townships to sue, reduce the expert findings on their building project to insignificance, and quote interminable sentences from past judicial decisions, which were canceled out by the lawyers for the plaintiffs with quotations from other judicial decisions. I learned some (to me) new words.

We let it pass. That, after all, is jurisprudence. Possibly I permitted myself a soft-spoken comment: "Absurd." But when after several "whereas" clauses the lawyer for the *Land* declared, "The theoretical danger of the installation is beyond the scope of the planning authority of the townships!," Dörte flung away her inhibitions and shouted: "Call that democracy! A nuclear state! That's what it's coming to!"

Evidently the judge thought this disturbance admissible, for he did not admonish the disturber. On the contrary, he let the trial take its course. Accordingly, Dörte Peters and I will learn in a few days that the promoters of the Brokdorf nuclear plant will be granted a first partial permit to start building a pressurized water reactor, cooled with Elbe water. And if, as Dörte and I do not doubt, this decision is put into effect with comparable single-mindedness, then in our film the location designated as "Elbe dike at Brokdorf with fenced-in building site" will have changed before we start shooting and the substance of Dörte's shout "A nuclear state! That's what it's coming to!" will have been confirmed.

Not only the promoters of the nuclear power plant, but Schlöndorff and I as well, will have to reckon with demonstrations and police action. While Harm and Dörte on the Elbe dike quarrel over Yes-to-baby No-to-baby, the construction site previously said to be peaceful, almost idyllic, will be crisscrossed by giant trucks and overarched by building noise. Henceforth, in facing up to their own specific headbirth, they will have to battle noise and confront another, a nuclear, headbirth; for ever since the mighty head of the god Zeus was got with child, the head of man has at all times been pregnant: something has always been growing, maturing; concepts have at all times been taking form. When Harm and Dörte have their preplanned trip to Asia behind them, they will fly back with their foreknowledge: Brokdorf is growing, whereas our child is again, is still, a wind egg.

At last they are flying at an altitude of eleven thousand meters through the likewise flying night. Their first meal—curried chicken with rice—and the first fueling stop (Singapore) are behind them. They would really like to sleep, but Dörte reads the novel—now a gift—down to the hideous massacre at the end, and Harm, who actually wanted to jot down travel impressions—the Cave of Bats, the gamelang music—but has already been sucked in by the inexorable election campaign, jots down topics for his speeches: The unprincipled opposition. Why Strauss is not a fascist but is nevertheless a danger. What safeguard requirements will have to be met before it will be acceptable to grant the Brokdorf pressurized water reactor a second construction permit. And uneasy thoughts about the world protein deficit. He tries to calculate the relationship between deaths from starvation and the rising price of soybeans. Fluctuations at the Chicago Board of Trade determine life and death. Dörte reads. Harm scribbles figures.

Both, he after a third beer, are tiredly wide awake when the movie screen is unrolled at the head of the cabin (movies are offered, at an extra charge, on long-distance flights). It's to be a western. Dörte and Harm decline the earphones. For them the film runs along soundlessly. But they are able (free of charge) to read what they please into it: their desires, their two filmed lives, both tragic.

She mixes scenes from *Love and Death on Bali* into the long-suffering western, which is never at a loss for action. He represses John Wayne and sees himself embroiled in partisan struggles on Timor. Dörte acts in the film version of Vicki Baum's novel. Both have leading parts. She swathed in a sarong, he in battle dress. And Wenthien's ghost is active in both, in one spooking through the palace of the Balinese prince, in the other following the trail of the arms smugglers. He helps Dörte spend the night with the rajah, he knows where Harm will at last find his school friend, good old Uwe. The innermost rooms of the palace. A cave in the mountains of Timor. True, the princely embrace, interrupted (just before the climax) by a Dutch artillery bombardment, dissolves into battle and flames; true, Harm is obliged, because the Indonesian armed forces have smoked out Uwe's headquarters, to pack up his liver sausage once again, follow his fleeing friend, and shoot his way out of the melee, but Wenthien, the intermediary and demiurge, always gives Harm and Dörte another chance. How Dörte (a Dutch renegade) gropes her way through the burning Pouri, the prince's palace, to spermatic happiness. How Harm finally (with bullet-riddled but miraculously still-fresh liver sausage) finds his dying friend. Over the heads of Dörte and Harm, while the western appears on the screen only intermittently, we see the double action. With them we see the Dutch infantry preparing to storm the palace, we see the ring of Indonesian soldiers closing in on Timor's last freedom fighters. We, like Dörte, are moved by the scene in which Dörte finds the mortally wounded prince. With Harm, we see Harm feeding the bullet-riddled liver sausage to his dying friend. On the brink of death, the rajah discharges life-giving seed into Dörte's womb. Only a bearded silhouette shows us good old Uwe munching away at the sausage as he is dying and finally, with a last "Thanks, Harm, thanks," giving up the ghost. We also hear the rajah breathing last words: "And so to Holland I give what has been taken from us: life. . . ." Over all this Wenthien holds the torch, the flashlight.

Exhausted, Harm and Dörte slump in their seats. Tears are rolling down her cheeks. He is panting. After the western and its two sets of fade-ins have flickered away, they have time for a few hours' sleep, which is interrupted by a fueling stop in Karachi and then broken again by a long-distance-flight breakfast, which is served while they are over the Mediterranean: mushy scrambled eggs. Then Dörte knits. Harm dozes. We see that the liver sausage has survived in their hand luggage. Could the smell now become so palpable as to play a minor role during the flight? Or is this the time, shortly before the landing in Hamburg, to have Dörte's ball of wool fall off her lap and roll down the aisle in the direction of the cockpit?

This could get too expensive. Schlöndorff would have to shoot Dörte's colonial war fade-ins and Harm's bloody guerrilla warfare on location and hire whole armies of extras. He'd also have to arrange for fluid transitions from wishful-dream film to western and from western to wishful-dream film, even if the return-flight sequence didn't take more than ten minutes. Five minutes might be better. I want my teacher couple to get home. I want them to find themselves in the same situation as we did after our long trip, not (in spite of my speculations) submerged in a billion Germans but mingled with a bare sixty million West German consumers.

That's plenty. That should be enough for us and the

world. They could perfectly well lose a little weight, write off a few million people, dispense with a corresponding number of second cars, concrete runways, kilowatt hours, climbers and dropouts, and you still couldn't call them impoverished or the country depopulated. Because, if we had a billion Germans (the Chinese figure) instead of a bare eighty million in two antagonistic states, it would be necessary, since the needs of the Germans would grow with their numbers, to multiply not only the number of their freeway kilometers and deepfreeze chests, the sheer bulk of their parliamentary bills, and their inventory of one-family houses, but also the litigious issues between the two states and between their equally peace-loving armed forces. Twelve times as many German choral societies, twelve times as many football games in both states, everything, including beer and sausage consumption, multiplied by twelve, lawyers, judges, doctors, clergymen, officials, civil servants, all multiplied by twelve; which would also apply to the occasionally smoothly running nuclear power plants of both states, as well as to those projected or under construction, so that, thanks to the increase in nuclear waste, proportionate growth would also be guaranteed in this sphere of progress.

For in our country everything is geared to growth. We're never satisfied. For us enough is never enough. We always want more. If it's on paper, we convert it into reality. Even in our dreams we're productive. We do everything that's feasible. And to our minds everything thinkable is feasible. To be German is to make the impossible possible. Has there ever been a German who, after recognizing the impossible, accepted its impossibility? Whatever it is, we'll do it! And all that multiplied by twelve!

In this light (to carry on with our speculations) the reunification of seven hundred fifty million Germans with roughly two hundred fifty million Germans would only be a matter of time. But time (ours) is running out, along with other raw materials. There isn't much left.

I made a mistake in banking on the snail. Ten and more years ago I said: Progress is a snail. The people who shouted at the time, "Too slow! Too slow for us!" may recognize (as I do) that the snail has slipped away from us, has hurried ahead of us. We'll never catch up. We're way behind. The snail is too quick for us. And if anyone (still) sees it crawling behind us, he should make no mistake: it will pass us by again.

That's an image. One more image. After Dörte Peters sets her wristwatch to local time while they wait for their luggage at the Hamburg-Fuhlsbüttel airport, Harm Peters says: "That's it. Now we're back in harness."

8

The village graveyard behind the Elbe dike with a view of overthere. Not far from Dannenberg, which is near Gorleben. On a sunny-cold December day. His landscape. Marshy meadows. Renovated by city people, the old half-timbered houses stand around like toys. The wife he has left behind. The desperately cheerful children. Berlin and Hamburg license plates: mourners from far away. Now that you are dead, I am aging more perceptibly. My courage, which was doing fine only yesterday, has furled several sails. Today, at your graveside, I heard (over the pastor's voice) the neighborhood cocks crowing good-bye to you.

It is hard surviving you, having to say from now on: As he rightly said even then . . .

Because our aims cloaked themselves in mist, you spoke diffusely. As soon as we see through the mists, we shall make you sound more to the point.

On the strength of your imprecise certainty you laugh and say: Freshly condensed mists will replace the transparent ones. No doubt about it.

So our longing for transparencies makes for cloaked progress.

While the cocks are still crowing and the pastor is doing his best, you say: Protest against the progressive powers is foreseen by the progressive powers.

What about your protest?

That, too. But my death was not on their program. The powers would have liked to keep me in their service. Surviving myself: I.

We must therefore become powerful in order to keep going as negative mists, long-lined poems, and short-lived poets. That would be very simple and hard to see through.

At this point, you say, the cocks laugh while, gathered around your grave, we make our faces.

Before my headbirth returns home in the form of Harm and Dörte Peters and plunges vociferously into the election campaign, I must say a last farewell to Nicolas Born, who died of cancer (so they say) on December 7, 1979, not quite two months after our return from Asia.

While our factions were still squabbling over ends and means and defining what was feasible at the moment as the feasible, he began to narrate *The Dark Side of the Story* and was horrified by the literal exploitations of horror; his "discoverer's eye" saw realities distinct from facts, gained an intimation of fact-saturated falsification, and finally (already dying) disclosed it.

That was yesterday, the day before yesterday. I have no need to remember him. To me Nicolas Born is present: as we sat face to face in Berlin in the early sixties. I with the final draft of *Dog Years* behind me; he a young man unsure of his beginnings. He has come from the Ruhr, there's a Westphalian massiveness about him, as though he had slowed down by sheer force of will, as though having to keep the potential bursts of speed (which would later drive him this way and that way) under control, still under control. The successful author, the beginner—these are our roles. We talk—I cautioning, as it were, he accustomed to warnings—about the risk of being a writer.

For a long time he emanated calm—shaping an all-too-simple image. Born, the quiet, steady, silent peasant. Occasional outbursts and provocations came equipped with apologies and retractions. Thus his image remains imprecise and does not gain in precision when he lets himself go, shatters the prescribed immobility, and becomes the restless, busy, driven, always concerned, increasingly endangered Born: a flying body obsessed by fear of flying. Anticipating every sort of crash.

In other words, not simple. Not reducible to any of the proposed images. Why should he be! A man who in 1972 said, "Reality is confined to conversation. It blinds us to everything else," can't be characterized in a simple statement; and even in his poems, which are all I-poems, he remains a stranger to us, as he is to himself:

> If I am utterly empty now,
> That is the revenge of reality

—two lines to which, as though apologetically, he appends a five-line footnote:

> (I have again let myself
> be driven far afield, into the thought
> of a whole world without power
> in which one man's gain
> would not be another's loss.)

His utopia? The headbirth of an outsider, who neglects facts for wishes? He has no desire to be more precise. A friend who never changes but is often unlike himself, who speaks of himself and his unearthly realities in asides if at all. Superficially, in visible, palpable closeup, he is a practical sort: reliable in an everyday way.

The Berlin years: I see him at the weekly market in Friedenau, saddled with two children and a shopping bag. We settle for a quick beer at the Ratskeller. We talk to each other like workmen.

I see him at the Bundeseck, where pinball machines move the world. Excluded, he stands among the mimes of revolution. He wants to say something: Listen to me! But they hear only themselves.

I see him as he passes with us through the border control at Friedrichstrasse Station and we take a cab to Köpenick. We've got something with us. (His closely written papers.) We're going to read to one another. The people waiting for us are like us, uncertain, outsiders, intent on words and their shadows, imperturbably exalted.

But whether at the Bundeseck, in the market, or at midnight in the railway station, our conversations are conversations between friends, who remain friends after each broken-off conversation, because neither offends the other's privacy by coming too close. This chastity is his *sine qua non*. His affection is not all-inclusive. His love insists on withdrawal. In the middle of a sentence, he breaks off and leaves. That's unsatisfactory, damn it. He hasn't been exploited enough yet. One wants to get a court order for his return, to have Big Boss Death sent up for fraud. One wants him to be here again, giving more, giving everything; for his last offering, pain, came to us from a distance, apologetically.

Before we left the village church and the cocks crowed over grave and coffin, I said: "Nicolas Born is dead. I know of no consolation. We might try to carry on with his life."

But how, when the facts pass him by so noisily? Banner

headlines thick as flies. Brokdorf Case Lost. Oil Prices Rising. Even the Church framing resolutions on energy: Give us today our daily gas. . . . Day in, day out, Khomeini and his hostages. Carter sends threats. Disarmament through rearmament. Peace the balance of terror. On the other hand, since dying is no novelty in those parts, Cambodia has dropped out of the news just as the mass murder of the Vietnam Chinese did a while ago. Old stuff before it has even stopped happening. Same as ten years ago, when the daily television ration of deaths from Biafra was drowned out by hopes aimed at the seventies, to which we shall say good-bye at the stroke of midnight, this December 31. On the one hand, we shall say of them, and on the other . . .

You won't be there on New Year's Eve. You've canceled. But I won't let you go. I will take you, Nicolas, you and the cock's crow under the graveyard sky, with me into Orwell's decade. You shall not be spared my headbirth. With you I will look on at the end of August—I'm not banking on much future for us—as Harm and Dörte Peters land at Hamburg-Fuhlsbüttel and collect their luggage, as from the taxi that's taking them to Altona they see the posters clamoring for security, as they are threaded into the election campaign, unable, once arrived, to shout "No," to say, "Enough Finis Death" as you did, but kept breathless between construction phases, wedged between wage-price and price-wage spirals, harnessed to objective realities, plunged each day into all-time lows and lured by hopes behind which they think they see—guess what!—a principle.

You know what it is to push a stone uphill. When we bade you farewell, Ledig-Rowohlt, your old publisher, compared you to Camus. ("I leave Sisyphus at the foot of the mountain! Time and again we find his burden.") That's heroic. For which reason I regard Harm and Dörte as heroes. To be sure, the stones that have been foisted on them aren't so very big, but even in flat country their up-and downhill itinerary is absurd. I'll introduce them to you. Dörte may appeal to you; especially her "somehow" sentences—"We'll get it done somehow!"—should meet with your indulgence. And you'll also get to know Harm, a good fellow, who, apart from statistics and fact sheets, reads nothing but detective stories.

They've been traveling. Just as you were in Lebanon, where you saw everything and nothing, they have come from Asia, where they understood everything and nothing. Only they can't write. They have to be written. They have civil-service status and are not so very young. What they experienced ten years ago (their protest) and what (for all their activity) they experience no longer. How their problem—Yes-to-baby No-to-baby—is always being swaddled afresh. What, apart from doodads, they have brought home from Asia, and what they know in addition to what they knew before. How it is that they get along pretty well without passion and how by converting their love into partnership they've made it easy to handle. Why this couple is not unique but interchangeable, and what they should say in the movie during the taxi ride to Altona.

"Well," says Harm Peters, "it's just as I expected. Forests of posters. Helmsman Schmidt. Statesman Strauss. Security versus security."

"Nothing is secure!" Dörte is sure of that. "Everything's on the skids. They're all kidding themselves. Only the environmentalists. Look over there, the good old environmentalists!"

"They'll get Strauss elected," says Harm, "that's what."

"Hmm," says the taxi driver. "Back from a long trip, aren't you?"

118

"Asia," says Harm. "India," says Dörte.

"Seen 'em on TV," says the driver. "Compared with conditions out there, we're better off here."

What, in the film, should Harm and Dörte say to that? Should they back up this reliable vote for the Chancellor? Should they put on some ontheonehand-ontheotherhand idea? Or should they pay in silence, take the train to Itzehoe, and drag their Yes-to-ecology No-to-ecology quarrel from Pinneberg to Glückstadt, through the flat Krempermarsch and Wilstermarsch, very much as they dragged their quarrel about the negated and affirmed baby from Bombay via Bangkok to Bali? (At the moment he wants "to become a father finally, damn it all"; but she has decided—"Try and understand"—to go back on the pill.)

And how will their return to Itzehoe, which receives them in election-campaign war paint, shape up? Here Harm's kink could take hold of him; on emerging from the station, he could pull the liver sausage out of his suitcase and fling it. (He aims at a Strauss poster, but hits a Schmidt poster next to it.) "For you, Franz Josef! — Sorry, Helmut . . ."

Or I have them (still with sausage) go straight home, where they unpack: she her Hindu doodads, he his Balinese sea shells and stones.

Or they pick up their cat, who is boarding with Uwe Jensen's sister. And there Dörte bursts into tears, because her cat, gray on white paws, who might be called Dixie, has kittened in the meantime.

"Five of them," says Uwe's sister Monika. "Three days ago. They're still blind. Aren't they cute?" But Dörte's eyes are swimming. She doesn't want to be objective any more.

Or after a cut (and because their vacation is almost over) I put the teacher couple right back in school, where they are immediately submerged by pupils' questions: "So what does a Japanese motorbike cost in Djakarta?" "Are you finally pregnant, Frau Peters?"

Or after a quick sequence of crosscuts—the train to Itzehoe, the flat Wilstermarsch, the exploding liver sausage, the cat and litter of five, the question-firing pupils—I send them into the thick of the election campaign. I put them in beer halls. In Kellinghusen, Lägerdorf, Wilster, and Glückstadt. I have them both say what I shall say when the time comes: In spite of everything, we. Even if everything is on the skids. The lesser evil if nothing else. Because after all. And without détente the whole. The circumstances notwithstanding. For fear that. Under Strauss, however. Even the environmentalists should. Otherwise the. The coming crises. Which Schmidt, as so often in the past. Even if it means tightening. Playing dead won't!

You're out of it, Nicolas. You've left us your poem "Safeguarded," which I, before the pastor did his best and the cocks crowed, read aloud for us: ". . . Life's walk-ons and walk-offs. Drip-fed by the systems . . ." That is still true. That can be quoted eternally from the sonnets of Gryphius. "And so we are driv'n away, as smoke by wind is driven." For Gryphius and Born, both in undying words, see the end of time coming.

Gryphius's apocalypse didn't come. Merrily people went on living murderously. Nor—you know it, Nicolas—will Born's end come. Murderously we'll survive and be merry. We shall adapt, defend, accommodate ourselves, and take safety measures. We will want to chuck it all and reproduce; and in the end (when the film is over) so will Dörte and Harm.

I am not chucking it. Every time I try, I (only seemingly elsewhere) slip back into my old commitments from a different direction. My down-at-heel escape shoes. To be present again, I often have to take a running start from remote centuries. There once was: there once is. There will have been once again. I'm curious about the eighties: a meddling contemporary. All right, I whistle in the woods. I dream heroic dreams. I push the downward-striving stone uphill, quoting all the while. I travel and take myself along. Back from Peking, I write German main and subordinate clauses in rough, second, and final draft. I'm counting on an audience that won't listen. No safe-guards will help me. My labors won't do your growth a bit of good. Because when I cast pearls before the Germans (as tested in China), speak of German literatures as *our* miracle (true enough, by comparing them with other miracles that have already begun to crumble), I can demonstrate the solidity of ours, but the Germans don't know themselves in this light, they don't want to.

They always insist on being terrifyingly more or pathetically less than they are. They can't leave anything alone. On their chopping block everything gets split. Body and soul, practice and theory, content and form, spirit and power—all so much kindling that can be put into neat piles. Life and death as well; with alacrity (or regrets) they banish their living writers; for their dead authors they plait wreaths assiduously and make a show of grief. They maintain their monuments, as long as the expense seems justifiable.

But we writers are indestructible. Rats and blowflies who gnaw at consensus and shit on the newly laundered tablecloth. Think of us all on Sunday afternoon when (if only in the crossword puzzle) you go looking for Germany: the dead Heine or the living Biermann, Christa Wolf over there, Heinrich Böll over here, Logau and Lessing, Kunert and Walser; put Goethe next to Thomas, and Schiller next to Heinrich, Mann; lock up Büchner in

Bautzen and Grabbe in Stammheim; hear Bettina when you hear Sarah Kirsch, find Klopstock in Rühmkorf, Luther in Johnson, Gryphius's vale of tears in the dead Born, and my idylls in Jean Paul. Anyone else I can think of down through the ages. Don't omit a single one. From Herder to Hebel, from Trakl to Storm. Forget about borderlines. Just so the language is spacious. Be rich in a different way. Skim off the profit. For (transcending the barbed wire) we have nothing better. Only literature (with its inner lining: history, myths, guilt, and other residues) arches over the two states that have so sulkily cut themselves off from each other. Let them persist in their antagonism—they can't help it—but impose this common roof, our indivisible culture, on them, lest we continue to stand in the rain like fools.

Both states will resist, because they live on antagonism. They don't want to be smart like Austria. They have to go on demarcating their Beethoven from our Beethoven (who lies in Vienna). Theirs and ours: every day they expatriate Hölderlin.

I'll talk about it in the election campaign: ignoring Strauss, but challenging Schmidt to do the one thing we can still do.

Set up a National Endowment, for instance. In 1972 the idea emerged in Brandt's program of government. In no time it became a bone of contention among the *Länder*. Since then nothing, only a bothersome item in the budget. To the opposition only the location mattered. The government's cowardly position: Let's show the other fellow up. More important was the economy, wage scales—and hunting down radicals. The inquiries of artists and their organizations brought no results but travel expenses. Ignorance carried over from year to year. Helplessness carried over into the next decade.

Today I realize that the task is beyond the means of the Federal Republic—or of the Democratic Republic alone. Only together—the way they concluded their Veterinary Pact, the way they regulate their highway tolls, that is to say, painstakingly in line with Gauss's law, and time and again foiled by the brinkmanship of world politics—would they be able to lay the foundations of a National Endowment, which would at last make it possible for us to understand ourselves and for the world to see us in a different and no longer terrifying light.

Such a National Endowment would have room for many things. The Prussian cultural heritage, cantankerously claimed by both states, would find its place. The chaotically dispersed cultural vestiges of our lost Eastern provinces could, if assembled there, help us to learn why those provinces were lost. There would be room for the contradictory trends in the arts of today. Exemplary works could be brought together from the richly varied wealth of the German regions. Not that the two states and their *Länder*, jealously attached as they are to their patrimony, should be impoverished. What needs to be created is not a monster museum, but a place where every German can look for himself and his origins and find questions to ask, not a mausoleum but an accessible meeting place—accessible through two entrances, for all I care (and provided, as befits a German institution, with plenty of exits). Yes, cry the slyboots, but where? As far as I'm concerned, in the no man's land between East and West, on Potsdamer Platz. There, at this one point, the National Endowment could neutralize that enemy of all cultures, the wall.

I hear loud cries: But that's impossible. They want to be by themselves, same as we do. Those people over there won't touch it. Or if they do, at what price? What's this, give them an equal voice? But they're much smaller and they're not a real democracy. And now, after all these

123

years, you want us to recognize them as a sovereign state? What exactly do we get in return? Ridiculous, two states, one nation. And a cultural nation at that. What can you buy for that?

Admitted. It's a wide-awake daydream. (Another headbirth.) I'm well aware that I'm living in a land of culturally active barbarism. Depressing figures can be cited to show that in both German states, more cultural substance has been ruined since the war than was destroyed during the war. Both here and over there, it is true, culture has been subsidized. Over there they fear the autonomous character of the arts; over here the artist is stood in the corner because of his "reservations." At the Social Democratic party congress, held on December 4 in Berlin, when Helmut Schmidt delivered a well-thought-out two-hour address, with which I, too, was impressed, he dealt with everything under the sun, but his only mention of culture was a list of European centers and industrial zones. And when in his speeches Erich Honecker* goes into production targets, there is always reason to fear that he will speak of cultural workers and their unmet quotas.

Why am I speaking here (and will soon be speaking in the election campaign) of something that troubles few Germans, although so many talk themselves blue in the face whenever the subject of Germany and German culture comes up? Because I know better. Because our literary tradition calls for such defiance, however powerless. Because it should be said. Because Nicolas Born is dead. Because I'm ashamed. Because what's wrong with us is neither material nor social, but an emergency of the spirit. And because my two teachers with civil-service status are stultified by their specialized knowledge, which breaks

---

* The head of government of the German Democratic Republic, i.e., East Germany. —Ed.

124

down into facts, tables, summaries, and fact sheets. Harm and Dörte have furnished their vacuum with card files. They flail about, submerged by data. At their beck and call: everything and nothing. "We ought to, we need to; it must be possible." Whenever they climb up on the Elbe dike at Brokdorf and look into the distance, they want to save the world. They catch on to every possible riddle but they don't understand themselves (in their medium, German dimension).

What has changed? Just that the cat has kittened? Now they're home, but Asia is striking back, whether he is speaking in half-full beer halls or she addressing groups of housewives. Both refuse to play the "polarization game." Since the environmentalists have nothing to offer but their negative stance, Harm and Dörte, she hesitantly, are determined to ask them "hard questions": About disarmament through rearmament. About guaranteed pensions. About job security. About security in general. But because they, too, find only soft answers to hard questions, their succinct reports tend to take on global dimensions.

"Of course," says Harm in Wilster, "our goal remains full employment. But we can't be sure of meeting the energy requirements of the eighties without the collaboration of the Third World."

"The free-market economy," says Dörte to an audience of housewives in Glückstadt, "should remain the foundation of our democratic order. But our day-to day consumer habits must take into account the rice shortage in Indonesia."

And when the two Asian travelers have talked themselves into a lather, when they are globally steamed up, when Harm has quoted from Brandt's *New Economic Order*, when Dörte has cited catastrophic figures from the papers of the Club de Rome, Dr. Konrad Wenthien, that tour guide and wonder-working guru, though long since written off as "too comical for words," mucks up their omnilaterally hedging speeches.

Then Dörte, who has just issued an appeal to reason, invokes "India's inalterably fatalistic structures"; and Harm, whose election slogan "Fear is a poor adviser" has just resounded, frightens the (all things considered) impressive crowd of cement workers in the suburb of Lägerdorf with his prognosis: "In the course of the eighties Asia will discharge its demographic pressure and flood the European continent. I see them by the thousands, by the hundreds of thousands, silently trickling in, and here, yes, here in Itzehoe, in our very midst. . . ."

So it seems that masses will have to be moved in our film. While Harm Peters puts his visions of horror into words and Dörte Peters escalates the world protein deficiency more and more terrifyingly, Schlöndorff has to round up extras, enrich the beer halls of the Wilstermarsch and the women's-club rooms of Glückstadt with Indians, Malays, Pakistanis, and Chinese, with Asia's overflow, until Harm and Dörte find themselves applauded by predominantly foreign audiences, while what's left of the native Germans, intimidated, lose themselves in the enthusiastic mass.

This I see as a sequence of rapid cuts. From sentence to sentence the two speakers conjure up the dreaded *Völkerwanderung* so graphically—"They come individually, they come in large families"—that in the end the hall is inhabited exclusively by New Europeans, for whom it has become too small: "Industrious, hard-working folk, frugal, quick to learn . . ." Only the waiter and the two waitresses seem to be of German stock.

And then, at both election meetings, Dr. Wenthien makes his appearance as co-speaker. In every language at his command, Hindi, Tamil, Indonesian, even in Mandarin Chinese, he proclaims the new world order: "The continents have joined into one family. Southeast and Northwest are one. Willingly—indeed, as we now see, happily—Europe is dissolving into Asia. . . ."

Flowers are thrown. Sticks of incense cloud the speaker's desk in mist. Off to one side a gamelang orchestra is playing. Wenthien's speech fosters harmony: "Thus rejuvenated, the German people will at last be a multitude. As a nation of many peoples, we will . . ."

Then, after an abrupt cut, dull reality prevails: Dörte admits to the well-fed Itzehoe housewives that after a long inner struggle she has decided not to support the environmentalists but (with critical reservations, of course) the Socialist-Liberal coalition: "That Bavarian boor* is no alternative!" Harm concludes his speech to the Lägerdorf cement workers with the sentence "In view of the crises to be expected during the eighties, we cannot afford the risk of Strauss or Albrecht!" Both are requited by adequate applause. The housewives pour themselves some more coffee. The cement workers call for beer. Only the waiters and waitresses seem foreign.

Our election campaigners are tired. Quite possibly, when they get home, he or she finds truth in the adage "Democracy is a damn strenuous business." Dörte swathes herself in an Indian sarong. Harm stands over his sea shells. They have quietly slipped away from their meetings. Only now do they make a decision that they ought to have made a week ago, when freshly back from Asia, but Dörte was dead set on granting the gray cat on white paws a little maternal happiness.

Only one kitten out of the litter of five will find a taker. The other four are too many. Uwe Jensen's sister

---

* Franz Josef Strauss. —ED.

127

will take one kitten. Because Harm assured her, "Your brother's doing all right on Bali, and man, was he happy with that liver sausage!" she has managed to convince her Erich, who had come out against a house cat: "After all, we haven't any children. A kitten will bring some life into the place."

Harm does the rest. He does it discreetly in the bathroom of the prewar apartment. The gush of water is heard, nothing more. He comes back with a plastic bag which (possibly along with the still-present liver sausage) he stuffs into a garbage bag. "They'll take it away tomorrow," he calls out.

Dörte sits tearless in her sarong. She is playing some Indian music on the phonograph. The gray cat pads about the room on white paws. She meows. Dörte says: "I'm afraid, Harm. Of us, of everything."

Between public readings in Stuttgart and Lohr I read the rough draft of *Headbirths* to Volker Schlöndorff in Marktheidenfeld, a Franconian town that I visited ten years ago in the course of the "Progress is a snail" election campaign. We were sitting in a tavern on the bank of the Main over a jug of Franconian wine. A few of the guests were startled by my *sotto voce* reading, but they tolerated us.

I adumbrated the end, which was still lacking, and filled in gaps as I went along: "Here I need a suitable quotation for the brochure of the Sisyphus Tourist Bureau. . . ." (I later decided on the sentence "The absurd man says yes, and his labor will know no end.") Volker showed me color photos of Java, street scenes, children. They were so good that everything looked artificial, as in nature.

Damn it! How can we mess up the aesthetics of color photography? It makes everything lovely, clear, smooth, acceptable. Fear, for instance. Dörte's fear, Harm's fear, ours. Fear isn't colored; it's gray. In resorting to color, we let a product of the film industry beguile us into brilliant falsifications. (The news of Born's death had reached me the day before.)

So let's say no to the products of industry. Reject these amazing inventions. Resolutely steer clear of the technological (human) development in the course of which everything feasible has been done. Let the feasible stumble over the touchstone of necessity. What the human (overgrown) head thinks up needn't be converted into action, needn't become reality. All headbirths, including mine, are absurd. That's why Sisyphus refuses a truck with four-wheel drive. He smiles. He doesn't want to accelerate his stone.

Impossible? We're already too dependent on headbirths that have cut loose and gone on developing on their own. Ever since Zeus. They perpetuate themselves without ovulation or effusion of sperm. Computers say of themselves: We belong to the third generation. There's no safeguarding against fast breeders. New early-warning systems make new rockets obsolete, whereupon young rockets render new early-warning systems ineffectual. I know nothing about genetics, but genetics knows about me. I haven't the faintest idea about microprocessors, which wouldn't give a hoot for my idea anyway. My protest against data banks has been banked. The bank thinks me. After the human head engendered (because it was feasible) brains, which then evaded its control, the liberated, autonomous, and soon enfranchised brains will (because it's feasible) shut down the human head. Then at last it will rest and let us rest.

For the present, it's still thinking away. With paternal pride (and only a little maternal worry) following the leaps of its headbirths into the proving ground of the eighties. How quickly they learn! How easily, before even mastering "Mama" and "Papa," they babble "self-realization." And how quickly, dropping Mama and Papa, they will realize themselves: more quickly and rigorously than Harm and Dörte, who all of ten years ago at the university in Kiel spoke of self-realization at the sit-in and in leaflets.

"Serve, conform. We are all cogs in the systems we ourselves devised. . . ." That, I said to Volker Schlöndorff in Marktheidenfeld, could logically be said by Dr. Wenthien, whereupon Harm and Dörte say No, just as they say No to the baby, to whom they actually say Yes, and whom they actually want. They are both looking for a new definition of progress. Because (out of habit) they want to be progressive. A turnabout would easily be misinterpreted, and they've never practiced standing still. "I'm beginning to feel afraid myself," says Harm. "All we've been doing is running after someone, I don't know whom."

They are standing on the Elbe dike near Brokdorf, watching—for since the Schleswig court dismissed the complainants' complaint, construction work in keeping with the first partial authorization has begun—the great autonomous, self-realizing Yes grow. The Yes to progress. The perpetually self-perpetuating Yes. The Yes to the eighties. Big Brother's Yes, somewhat, but not excessively, incommoded by Orwell's never-recanted No.

Nicolas Born, how long you have already been dead! The dates since then have passed so quickly. I've just put a fresh sheet of paper into the typewriter; I want to get rid of them—of these headbirths.

9

The Chinese women couldn't get over her way of holding the needles. Rather shy as a rule, they just had to see from close up the Central European method of knitting. (If women were organized into a mighty International of Knitting Women, there would soon be nothing left for men but to look on.) For in spite of all obstacles and interruptions, the muffler in graduated earth colors that Ute had started knitting during our train trip from Shanghai to Kweilin, and which had lengthened during our journey through Asia, was finished at Christmas, because Ute had stuck to the thread, while my thought-threads had lost themselves in the far-flung muck of the present and are still in a hopeless tangle, despite my efforts to track them down.

Minor catastrophes keep passing themselves off as news, as though this last year of the seventies had hastened in its final moments to square its accounts: after an epileptic fit Rudi Dutschke, aged thirty-nine, drowns in his bathtub. A late denouement of an old plot. An assassination attempt fomented by countless headlines results, ten years later, in fatal consequences. Even then people were talking of medium-term perspectives. Superannuated footage is shown on TV: his oratorical fervor.

What makes me sad? A revolutionary out of the German picture book. How he was carried away by his wishes. How his ideals escaped him at a gallop. How his visions degenerated into paperbacks. How he became good old Rudi—quiet, friendly, in need of help—and ended up with the environmentalists. They let him speak—regardless of contradictions.

When Marx speaks through Melanchthon: it was probably the special mixture of Protestant eloquence and wishful socialism that enabled Rudi Dutschke to state his message in such ambiguous circumlocutions. Nowadays it's Rudolf Bahro who keeps the Messianic element in German politics fresh and green: faith that refuses to be put off by reality. Because it fears no borderline, not even the deadly-secure wall, this tradition that is developing in both states will preserve the semicolon as the emblem of German contemplativeness—however industriously the one and the other state may plant forests of mutually antagonistic exclamation marks.

For a short time I regarded Rudi Dutschke as a recognizable adversary; then, when he became demagogic, as an indistinct one. In the late sixties, the struggle against him and his enemies was not without danger: mutual hatred made for an alliance of the left and right against the center. Later, Dutschke had to be on his guard against his supporters. Many (but not he) put his appeal for a "march through the existing institutions" into practice and went to work for the government.

I wonder how Harm and Dörte Peters, who saw and heard Rudi Dutschke in the course of a mammoth demonstration in Berlin, who joined forces with him for two semesters, are taking his death. Like me, who have aged with the years, they, who (contrary to their expectation) have not remained young, have seen the terminal news item. Has it shaken them? Do they allow themselves to be shaken? Does he say, "Damn it all!" Does she say, "In the bathtub—that's not right for him"? Could it be that eight months after Rudi Dutschke's death—they've just come back from Asia—Harm still has a newspaper photo (with the date written in by hand) pinned up over his desk? And has Dörte been able to shed tears over the pregnant wife he left behind him and his two children? Or do they, in the spirit of the times, pooh-pooh all that, the ideas and heroes of their protest and student days?

Possibly Harm Peters says: "Politically speaking, Rudi was dead even before they tried to murder him." And I hear Dörte Peters: "He sure could sweep you off your feet. But afterward, when I read what he had said, I couldn't make head or tail of it. I'm frankly puzzled about my enthusiasm when he . . ."

They're detached, or claim to be. I don't believe them. They say they didn't really mean the things they had found it so easy to parrot after him: "Character masks and that kind of thing . . ." They insist that they had had their reservations when they came out for this and against that. And besides, they say, the whole movement was different in Kiel: much more disciplined.

Harm and Dörte can't admit that with Dutschke's death something died in them: a certain feeling, a general outlook; for since then (as both say) they have been "sensitized" to worldwide injustice, but less and less to the injustice around the corner.

That's another thing they should talk about—in Bombay or under hotel palms on Bali. Wherever they ought to fall silent, they are tensed in conversation. "I admit it," Dörte might say in the Klong Toei slum, "Dutschke's death left me rather cold when I saw it on the news program. But he did sensitize us to this here—the global picture, I mean, the Third World and everything that's wrong in such places."

Promptly as Harm agrees with his Dörte—"Yes, of course, he showed us certain important contexts"—he claims to have been sensitized before knowing Dutschke: "About the North-South differential and all that—about us getting richer and them poorer. We just didn't want to listen."

They both remember their beginnings inaccurately. Too much present has got in the way: "It sends you up the wall." Rather sorry for themselves—but ironic about their self-pity: "Man, do we whine!" They deplore their sins of omission but debit them to the account of altered circumstances or—as Dörte says—"social constraints." This they do in all situations and places, no matter how remote. Seldom has a generation exhausted itself so quickly; either they crack up or they stop taking risks.

And so, since the circumstances and constraints of the Asian journey admit of no clear answer, the Yes-to-baby No-to-baby question is subjected to new upsets. True, they agree (during pauses in the election campaign) that as soon as Harm's mother is unable to manage on her own in Hademarschen, she should be sent to an old-people's home ("She herself says she'd prefer it to moving in with us"). But when Harm throws Dörte's pills into the john, demands to know "what's what," and lights into his Dörte like a bull, first in the bathroom and then in the bedroom, she says toward the end of the film what I had jotted down for the beginning: "It's no good, Harm. Now everything depends on the elections. Under Strauss there's no way I'll bring a child into the world."

It's time for the film to stop. Only school and the election campaign go on. The outcome of the latter is unknown to me. Just as the year 1980, until it dawns tomorrow, is altogether shrouded in mist, open at most to speculation. The latest news puts Soviet troops in Kabul. Something is contracting (as though out of control). Quick, find Afghanistan in the atlas. Madness spreads with perfect logic. The two great powers could be in this mood or that mood. Or an error in translation could have consequences. Crisis teams—every bit as mindlessly worried as I am: if there's a war, Schlöndorff and I won't be making a movie—will meet all over the world. They play the role they have learned: graduated deterrence. They can count to three. Sarajevo, Danzig . . .

Let's hope the weather holds. Ute and I have invited company. For New Year's Eve. We're supposed to have brisket of beef with green sauce. Preceded by fish: flounder, it goes without saying.

After their last classes at the Kaiser Karl School (KKS for short), Harm and Dörte Peters got into their old VW, which they've kept in shape since they started teaching, intending, before the election campaign hullabaloo starts up again, to go home for a quick meal in the prewar apartment full of travel souvenirs, to their cat, gray on white paws. On a little-traveled side street (Dörte is driving) a small boy runs out in front of the car, but (except for a jamming on of brakes) nothing happens.

It's a Turkish boy, nine or ten years old, who's lucky again and laughs. Other Turkish boys are waiting for him, and together they celebrate his survival. Now from side streets and backyards, from all directions, come more and more children, all foreign. Indian, Chinese, African children, all cheerful. They fill the street with life, wave from windows, jump from walls, innumerable. All cheer for the little Turk, who has been lucky again. They crowd around him, run their hands over him. They run their hands over the well-preserved VW where sit our childless teacher couple, not knowing what to say in German.